95 NN
01

PERSONS FROM PORLOCK

Louis MacNeice

Persons from Porlock

AND OTHER PLAYS FOR RADIO

WITH AN INTRODUCTION

BY W. H. AUDEN

British Broadcasting Corporation

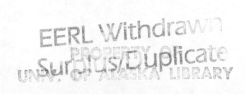

Published by the
British Broadcasting Corporation
35 Marylebone High Street
London, W.1
First published 1969
© The Estate of Louis MacNeice, 1969
SBN 563 08452 9
Printed in England by The Broadwater Press Ltd

Contents

Foreword

Louis MacNeice wrote a considerable number of radio plays on a wide variety of subjects, and it is quite impossible in one volume to give an adequate representation of the whole range of his work.

As a preliminary to making this selection, I asked myself: 'Out of the various themes he treated, which were so well suited to radio that I cannot imagine them being as successful in any other medium?'

I began, therefore, by excluding his dramatisations of already existing prose works, of the *Njal Saga*, for example, and the scene of *Trimalchio's Feast* from the *Satyricon*. These seem to me extremely well done, but this selection is a book to be read, and since good translations, both of the *Saga* and of Petronius, exist, I think the interested reader will prefer to go to the originals.

The most striking difference between radio drama and the ordinary stage play is that in the former everything the characters say is heard primarily as a soliloquy. In a stage play the audience 'overhear', so to speak, the remarks which the actors they see address to each other; in a radio play each remark is heard as addressed directly to the listener, and its effect upon the invisible characters in the play is secondary.

Then, unlike the stage play, the radio play, like the movie, permits of almost instantaneous changes in place and time – the Aristotelian Unities are irrelevant to the medium – and a large cast is economically possible. The Elizabethan stage without scenery or proscenium permitted the Elizabethan dramatist, if he so wished, to write, as a modern dramatist cannot, short scenes, but only fairly short, since it takes time for the actors to make their entrances and exits: in a radio play a scene can be only a few seconds long.

This means, I think, that radio drama is an excellent, perhaps the ideal, medium for 'psychological' drama, that is to say the portrayal of the inner life, what human beings privately feel and think before and after they perform a public act. For its principal characters, therefore, it demands men and women who are by nature self-conscious and articulate: Hamlet is more suited to radio than Fortinbras.

MacNeice's last play, *Persons from Porlock*, seems to me a magnificent example of such a psychological drama. It covers more than twenty years of the life of Hank, a would-be painter. From the outside, these years are mostly a record of frustration and worldly failure. He starts out with the hope of becoming a 'pure' painter. He fails. He becomes a commercial artist but preserves too much artistic conscience to succeed as one. He takes to the bottle, and his girl friend leaves him. He starts painting again and is reduced to beggary.

(There is a suggestion that these paintings of his last phase procured him post-humous fame.) In addition, however, to his interest in painting and women, and his alcoholism, he is enchanted by the idea of exploring caves: under-ground, and only underground, he feels happy and himself. And it is in a cave that he meets his death. I shan't spoil the reader's pleasure by further descrip-tion. I would only point out that Hank's death is a good illustration of a scene that would only be possible in a radio play. As he is dying, various characters who have played a part in his life appear to him and speak, helping him to arrive at a deeper self-knowledge. If one tries to imagine this scene in a stage play, one realises that it would not work. Firstly, while in the radio play one knows that the other characters are thoughts inside his head, if brought on to the stage they would be visibly external, so that the audience would be puzzled to know – a fatal dramatic flaw – whether they were 'real' or tiresomely 'sym-bolic'. Secondly, a dying man cannot 'do' anything: he can only lie there motionless, and on stage a motionless figure is an undramatic bore.

Several of MacNeice's best radio plays – I wish I had room to include more of them – were dramatised fairy-tales, some, like *The Heartless Giant*, tra-ditional, others, like his best-known play, *The Dark Tower*, and *Queen of Air and Darkness*, his original creation.

Again, the medium of radio seems peculiarly suited to the fairy-tale. To be-gin with, since the world of fairy-tales is a Secondary World where the laws, inhabitants, events are utterly different from those of the Primary World of our public experience, every fairy-tale is, in a sense, a 'psychological' drama, for it deals with our imagined experiences, not our actual ones. Secondly, the fairy-tale world is full of supernatural characters, embodied natural forces, talking animals, and magical transformations. On a visible stage these are very difficult, if not impossible, to make convincing. In the case of a talking animal, for example, the audience is always conscious that it is a human being dressed up as an animal, and it is not possible before the eyes of an audience for a beast to change into a man or vice versa. The disembodied voices of radio, on the other hand, can present such things convincingly, for the imagination of the listener is not spoiled by any collision with visual reality.

In two of the plays I have selected, *Enter Caesar* and *They Met on Good Friday*, MacNeice deals with historical subjects, in the first with Julius Caesar's rise to power, in the second with the complicated and ambiguous relations between the viking and the native inhabitants in Ireland during the tenth and eleventh centuries.

In considering with what elements in political history radio drama is best capable of dealing, it may be helpful to think first about the medium which is its antithesis, the old silent movie. In the purely visual world of the latter, the audience can tell from the physical appearance of the characters, and what they are wearing, who is physically strong or weak, beautiful or ugly, rich or poor, who gives orders and who obeys them. But if the director wishes to indicate that this character is morally good and that one morally bad, he has to resort to type-casting, which everyone knows is a fake; in real life, villains can look like saints and vice versa. The camera can convey the emotions felt by the characters to the degree that these are visibly manifest in facial expressions or gestures, scowls, grins, laughter, tears, etc, which in practice means their emotions in critical situations. When their faces are still, their feelings remain unknown. If it is essential for the audience to know what somebody *says*, the director has to resort to the caption which is necessarily very brief and elementary: nobody can make a speech or conduct an argument. As for the thoughts of a character, the camera can tell us nothing whatsoever. On the other hand, the camera is superbly equipped to show the simultaneous actions of a large number of people, as on a battlefield or at a State triumph or funeral. In short, a silent movie on an historical subject can show us very vividly what actually happened, but it can tell us scarcely anything about why it happened.

With the medium of radio drama, it is just the other way round. All physical action and all mass behaviour has to take place, so to speak, 'off-stage' as conventional noises, clashing of weapons, cheers, boos, etc. But, because it makes us hear what characters say, even in a dialogue with each other, as a soliloquy, it can express better than any other medium the reasons people give themselves for taking this or that action.

In *Enter Caesar*, its hero never speaks a word. What we hear are a series of political discussions by others, both professional politicians and men-in-the-street about him. Is he a danger to them personally or to the State, or is he a saviour? Would it be good policy to support him or oppose him? In either case, what steps should be taken? The result, to my mind, is most interesting, dramatic, and, in the best sense of the word, educational. It gives those of us who are not, like MacNeice, classical scholars who have read all the historical documents, a clear understanding of the political and social conditions in the Roman Republic after Sulla's death which enabled Caesar to come to power.

It is melancholy to reflect, firstly, that Louis MacNeice is dead and can give us no more poetry, secondly, that, since the advent of television, radio drama is probably a dying art. A dramatic medium in which almost all the effect depends upon the spoken word offers unique opportunities to poets, and it will be a matter for regret if they are going to be deprived of it.

W. H. AUDEN

Enter Caesar

A study of the evolution and background of
the first great dictator of the modern type

First broadcast in the BBC Home Service on 20 September 1946 in Louis MacNeice's production with music by Elisabeth Lutyens; conducted by Warwick Braithwaite, and the following cast:

CENTURION	*Ivor Barnard*
SCHOOLMASTER	*Duncan McIntyre*
SULLA	*Esme Percy*
APOLLONIUS	*Malcolm Graeme*
CRASSUS	*Cyril Gardner*
POMPEY	*Laidman Browne*
CATULUS	*Ernest Thesiger*
BIBULUS	*Alexander Sarner*
CISALPINE GAUL	*Harry Hutchinson*
GABINIUS	*Roger Snowdon*
CICERO	*Cecil Trouncer*
CATO	*Mark Dignam*
CLODIA	*Grizelda Hervey*
CLODIUS	*John Chandos*
MILO	*Howard Marion-Crawford*

and members of the BBC Drama Repertory Company

Announcer Enter Caesar. Exactly two thousand years ago this summer the Roman legions first landed in Britain; the man who led them was Gaius Julius Caesar. For two thousand years since then he has been a subject of controversy. An idealist? A power-politician? An inspired statesman? A necessary evil? A warning to us or a model? The answer cannot be clear-cut. Caesar, like everyone else, can only be assessed against his historical background. The programme which follows will try to fill in that background. In 55 B.C. your ancestors watched with alarm a number of little ships approaching the coast of Kent. They were quite right to be alarmed. Those triremes in the Channel came from another world. Enter a New Order. *Enter Caesar!*

(musical effect; then simmer behind)

Centurion Ha! White cliffs. And a pack of blue savages on top of 'em.

(music effect and simmer behind)

And these damn tides are a puzzle. If it wasn't that I'm a centurion –

(quick musical effect)

I should be sick in my helmet. Puzzle? *We'll* give 'em puzzles.

(musical figure – heaving waves)

Those Britons will have to be brighter than me if. . . Look out, Britain. He's coming!

(up music – Caesar fanfare and clean out)

Schoolmaster 'His dismissis et ventum et aestum uno tempore nactus –' Wake up there, Jamie Fraser! Don't you know where we've got to? This is Caesar calling; I think you boys might listen.

Och, I know the Bellum Gallicum is a bore but it's better written than *Mein Kampf*. Now let's get on with our construing. 'His dismissis –' Yes, Logan, what is it?

What's the connection with Hitler? All right; close your books. I'll try and paint for you now the history of a dictator. One of the first and one of the best specimens. But remember this. You only get a dictator when things are an awful mess. And things at Rome were an awful mess in those days. Look at that map behind me. When Caesar was in his teens the Romans already ruled the whole of the Mediterranean. And how did they rule it? With a little gang of lairds who sat confabbing in Rome and didn't give a hoot for anyone's rights but their own. Corrupt as they make 'em and inefficient as well.

13

Aye, the whole show's bankrupt, boys. Politically, economically, socially, morally. So something had to snap. There was a left wing – it had been blethering for decades – that wanted revolution. Caesar himself began as a left-winger, a demagogue. But he took his cue from another dictator before him. Name of Sulla. An out and out conservative. In 82 B.C. when Caesar was barely twenty – but already married, they married early in those days – Sulla marched into Rome at the head of an army and started a reign of terror. That should be easy enough for you to picture; you're all big boys now, you can read your daily papers. A reign of terror, backed by marching men...

(*fade up orchestra, first few bars reminiscent of Horst Wessel, then twist into Legionary March and end triumphant*)

Cornelia But you must divorce me, you must! Pompey's divorced *his* wife. Sulla's orders are Sulla's orders, Gaius. Whenever I walk through the Forum and see those heads hanging up there – I wonder when yours will join them. You can't afford to be married to Cinna's daughter! It puts you on Sulla's death list. So sign the divorce *now*! It's no good, Gaius, waiting for him to die. Old and rotten though he is...

Sulla Whom the gods love die old; give me some more Falernian. My complexion can't be worse than it is but – Thank you, my dear fellow, thank you. Now what were you saying? Caesar?

Slave Yes, my lord; this pardon that you've just issued. Of course it is not my place to suggest that –

Sulla Nowhere's your place. You're a slave.

Slave I apologise very deeply.

Sulla But as secretaries go, you're good; help yourself to some wine. Why do you think I should not have pardoned Caesar?

Slave Caesar has disobeyed you.

Sulla He's only a boy. Most boys of that age are silly.

Slave Yes, my lord, but, if I may remind you, no other boy of that age is married to Cinna's daughter.

Sulla Cinna I have dealt with. His party I have dealt with. One stray son-in-law cannot affect the issue. When's that flute-girl coming?

Slave In an hour's time, my lord.

Sulla Good. And she only speaks Greek?

Slave I'm afraid so, my lord –

Sulla Afraid? I adore speaking Greek. She is not too skinny, I hope? That actress you brought me last week –

Slave It shall not occur again.

Sulla When I was young I lived in a tenement; all the girls there were skinny. Like Pompey's new wife that I gave him. Poor little Pompey the Great.

Slave My lord, if I might ask you –

Sulla Why did I ever call that young cub the Great? A baby name. Only a baby name. You and I know that the species is now extinct. No more great men – after me.

Slave All the same, my lord, Pompey –

Sulla Pompey has beautiful eyes but he is a parvenu. Yes – and he lacks imagination; *he'll* never make a rebel. As for that other young man, you saw how I dealt with him.

Slave Crassus?

Sulla I will not have my commanders dealing in real estate. If Crassus *must* make money, let him play his tricks in private. And remain a private person for the rest of his life. No, no, my dear, no more great men after me. The Republic from now on will be run by the Best People. But with plenty of safeguards. Hm?

Slave Indeed, my lord, your system of checks and balances –

Sulla A masterpiece, a masterpiece. It has made revolution impossible; there'll never be another Marius. The Senate are back in the saddle but no one Senator can ever climb too high. I have shackled Big Business, purged the law-courts, hamstrung the tribunate, gagged the popular Assembly. Yes – and frightened the stinking masses into eternal silence. In fact I have been very clever – and very lucky. When is that flute-girl coming?

Slave In an hour's –

Sulla Yes, yes, of course. You're really a very good secretary. Shall I let you into a secret? I'm freeing you in my will.

Slave Oh, my lord!

Sulla As soon as I die – and I shall die quite soon –

Slave I am so glad, my lord.

Sulla Glad?

Slave Oh, not that. I – I didn't for a moment, I –

Sulla Glad? When Sulla is dead? Ha! Ha! Even if you're not, my dear, plenty of others will be.

    (*music*)

Crassus So Sulla is dead? So much the better for that. Depriving me of my

15

command because it was lucrative. Now I can see possibilities. I shall get them to send me against the rebel Spartacus. I may not be Pompey the Great but –

Pompey I may not be Crassus the Rich but now that Sulla is dead the roads are open again. I shall get them to send me to Spain to beat that rebel Sertorius. When Sulla entitled me Great he little imagined – No matter; now for the Future!
(*Crassus' fanfare, and out*)

Crassus Soldiers! I thank you. You have done your duty. Spartacus the rebel is beaten. Italy is pacified. *Now* – we return to Rome!
(*cheering 'Crassus! Crassus! Crassus!' and Pompey's fanfare*)

Pompey My friends –
(*cheers*)
Thanks to you I have cleaned up Spain. I have defeated the rebel Sertorius. For five years you have fought in this barren country – but you have never faltered. You have shown yourselves true Romans. Let Rome reward you.

Crowd (*cheers – 'Pompey! Pompey! Pompey!'*)

Pompey (*close*) I shall see that Rome rewards you. You – and me.
(*fade up Legionary March from distance and behind*)

Voice A They're coming! They're coming!

Voice B Crassus from the South.

Voice C Pompey from the North.

Voice D What's going to happen now?
(*up March and to clean, strong close*)

Catulus The situation, gentlemen, is serious in the extreme. The late lamented Sulla, whatever his faults, was at least loyal to the Senate.

Crowd (*'hear! hear!'*)

Catulus The excellent constitution which Sulla established ten years ago has successfully weathered the attacks of all the young irresponsibles –

1st Senator Caesar, for instance.

Catulus Quite so. And talking of that young man with the long fringes on his sleeves, you remember that only recently he supported the agitation over the tribunate?

Bibulus Supported it with sticks and stones too.

1st Senator Yes, he's becoming quite a gang leader.

16

All	(*laughter*)
Catulus	Gentlemen!
1st Senator	I'm sorry, Catulus.
Catulus	Caesar, I agree, is merely a cause for laughter –
Bibulus	I don't know. He's being financed by Crassus.
2nd Senator	That's nothing new. If one has debts like Caesar's –
1st Senator	A purse full of cobwebs!
All	(*titters*)
Catulus	Gentlemen! Can we now drop this subject of Caesar and turn to the real danger?
	Pompey and Crassus are both approaching this city at the head of conquering armies. What is going to happen when they get here? I will not say that either of these gentlemen is actually hostile to the regime –
Voices	Of course not. Of course not.
Catulus	But I cannot help inquiring what will happen if either – or both – of them are hostile. Crassus after all is the champion of Big Business; he would like to remove the Sullan restrictions on finance.
Bibulus	Yes, but Crassus is jealous of Pompey.
1st Senator	And Pompey loathes Crassus.
2nd Senator	I don't blame him. A multi-millionaire is always rather disgusting.
All	(*laughter*)
1st Senator	My bet is that they'll fight it out with each other.
Catulus	Gentlemen! Time is short. I asked you here to my house to discuss a very possible situation. Supposing Pompey and Crassus sink their differences –
Bibulus	Most unlikely, Catulus.
1st Senator *2nd Senator*	} Most unlikely, most unlikely.
Catulus	But supposing they *do*? Supposing they both stand for consul? Supposing –
Bibulus	But Pompey's not qualified to stand.
Catulus	Allow me. Supposing they both are elected? As they will be – with armies behind them.
	(*cheering* – 'Pompey! Pompey!')
Bibulus	What's that cheering?
Catulus	That . . . is their armies behind them.
	(*mix with Crassus cheers; then out at peak*)
Crassus	Thank you, sir. I am glad we have cleared up those little differences.

17

Pompey So am I, Marcus Crassus. And it is arranged that we both keep our armies outside the gates?

Crassus Until the elections are over. And you are agreed about the Asiatic taxes?

Pompey I do not go back on my word.

Crassus Why, Pompey, who would imagine –

Pompey Crassus! To avoid misunderstanding between us, when we are joint consuls –

Crassus There should be no misunderstanding. We have only a year in office. We shall be far too busy.

(*up Forum music and behind*)

Voice E Well, what will those two do next?

Voice F Restoring the tribunate!

Voice G Reforming the law-courts!

Voice H Purging the Senate!

Voice J Bringing back the corn-dole!

Voice K Goody; goody; goody!

(*music out*)

Crassus Here you are, my dear Caesar. Pay it back when you like – and of course I'll charge no interest. That should cover your expenses but if you want any more – I'm not leaving Rome just yet. Why should I? Pompey's still here. His consulship seems to have tired him. Between you and me, I think he's not a politician. What a year, my dear Caesar, what a year. Every measure I proposed meant endless argument with him. The poor man doesn't really know what he wants, I believe. Of course he came round every time and we did get results. The Forum's a different place; Sulla must be turning in his grave. It's just the right moment in fact for you to enter the Senate; there's a future in politics again. But when they elect you quaestor – and today's little, er, transaction has made your election certain – take warning by Pompey and a tip from me. Be a good mixer, Caesar. And be a good showman. Not that I really think you need such advice.

(*fade up funeral march in distance and increase behind*)

Tough Come on, fellows, come on. Any more for the peep-show?

Lounger What are you talking about?

Tough The funeral, man, the funeral. Our new quaestor's aunt. Julia, you dunderhead. They say it's rich.

Freedwoman Yes – and you know what they tell me? In the procession he shows the bust of Marius.

Lounger No?

Freedwoman But it's true.

Lounger But that's unheard of. Marius is taboo.

Tough Ha! Ha! Ha! Tell that to Caesar.

Lounger But the nerve of that dressy young fly-by-night –

Tough Come on, you mugs, it's approaching; d'you want to miss it? D'you want to miss Caesar's speech? Come on! Up Aunt Julia!

(up march music, then fade out)

Catulus Disgraceful! Disgraceful! Making political capital out of a funeral. I had a stenographer there. Would you like to read it? Here, take it – but don't burst a blood vessel.

Bibulus *(reading)* 'Citizens, I come before you today bowed down with grief...' um...um...um...

Catulus Just unroll it a little.

Bibulus 'On my mother's side my Aunt Julia was descended from the ancient kings, on her father's side from –'

What! He can't have said that!

Catulus 'On her father's side from the immortal gods.' That's what he said, my dear Bibulus. My stenographers are accurate.

Bibulus Take it back. I refuse to read such stuff.

Catulus No, read it, read it. It throws considerable light on their new propaganda. My stenographer makes a note that whenever he mentioned Marius – and the other old radical leaders – the people shouted their heads off.

Bibulus The people, oh the people!

Catulus It's the fault of Pompey and Crassus. They opened the door to all this.

Bibulus Yes – and it was Crassus, I hear, who bought Caesar his quaestorship.

Catulus Of course it was. He wants a coalition between Big Business and the demagogues. But I've been talking to Cicero – a coming man, I think –

Bibulus Not one of us, Catulus.

Catulus Of course not – but we can use him. We must wean Cicero from Pompey, we must split Big Business and Crassus.

Bibulus And Caesar?

Catulus Oh, Caesar? You can forget about him till he returns from Spain – Time enough then to see what road he takes.

Cisalpine Well now, isn't it lucky you took the road you did? And the pleasure is mine to have entertained you in passing. I hope you'll forgive me saying so, as you're a Roman magistrate, but you're the first of the kind, Gaius Julius Caesar, that I've ever met who's understood our problems. Your people would call me a Gaul since I live north of the Po but, as you so rightly said, sir, Gauls or no Gauls, what we want is our rights. Which is more than those old diehards down in your Roman Senate – begging your pardon, sir, I know you're a senator too but it's clear to me you're different. That's why I and my friends up here will be keeping our eyes on you. The whole world needs reform and you're the kind to give it us. And I don't mind how you do it.

(fade up Forum music – a short passage – and out)

Pompey I'm sorry, Caesar, I tell you I don't really want it.

Gabinius Don't believe him, Caesar. Pompey the Great is not only great on the battlefield; he's great at effacing himself.

Pompey Gabinius, I –

Gabinius That was a joke, Pompey, but let us be serious. Since your consulate expired, you've been too retiring. Your friend Crassus has spent these last two years writing cheques as usual, pulling wires as usual, making friends as usual.

Pompey If you call them friends.

Gabinius That's as may be. Your case is, after all, different; Crassus has never had glamour. But glamour can fade, Pompey. It's time you came back into the torchlight.

Pompey I do not desire any torchlight. And to tell you the truth, gentlemen, I mean no aspersion on either of you personally, but – I find your platform too radical.

Gabinius That's as may be. Don't be so innocent, Pompey; think of the powers we're proposing. No Roman general in history will ever have had such powers.

Pompey I am aware of that. Out of all proportion to their object.

Gabinius Heavens, Caesar! Do you hear him? My dear Pompey, the pirates are merely a stepping-stone. Don't you see what we're driving at? As soon as my bill is passed, you go out to the Aegean and the Levant; you sweep the pirates off the seas. Well done; there you are in the East. Well, there's still a war on there – and the Senate have bungled it badly. Now the obvious man for that war is a man like you. And as there is no one like you –

Pompey Gabinius. I still don't like your proposal. It is a dangerous precedent. An extraordinary command is always open to abuse. If it is forced upon me, if it is the will of the country, I shall accept it. But under protest, Gabinius.

Gabinius Good. Then that's settled. And it *will* be the will of the country. I, as tribune, shall bring it before the Assembly and Caesar here will – er – organise the streets.

(*up Forum music, agitato, and into Pompey's fanfare*)

Catulus Disgraceful! Perfectly disgraceful! That law of Gabinius' last year was bad enough but this new bill that Manilius is bringing in . . .! I shall speak against it myself.

Bibulus It is your duty, Catulus. The radicals are going to make Pompey into a tyrant. And did you hear what I heard in the colonnade to-day? Your white hope, Cicero, is supporting the bill.

Catulus I know. I am deeply disappointed in him.

Bibulus What can you expect from a man without any background? What a greaty pity the people elected him praetor. I suppose he'll be consul next!

Catulus The people are all against us; Pompey's their idol, and the joint stock companies want their profits in Asia. And Caesar of course is supporting the bill too; he hopes to be aedile next year.

Bibulus The corruption of it all, the corruption! We must not lose this debate.

Catulus Of course we shall lose it, Bibulus.

Crowd (*fade up booing*)

Catulus People of Rome, I appeal to you! Let me at least conclude my speech in quiet. I have already perhaps said enough to prove –

Voice L You have said quite enough!

Crowd (*laughter and jeers*)

Catulus Romans! Romans! Where is your sense of order? Do you think that I have been speaking against Pompey.

Voice M Oh, no!

Crowd (*booing*)

Catulus I tell you I have nothing against Pompey. This is not a question of personalities. It is a question of principle. The bill under debate is a revolutionary bill. It will give too much power to one man. I do not care who that man may be – it is a dangerous precedent. It is a fatal precedent. I ask you therefore to reject it.

Crowd (*booing and fade out*)

Whisperer Hsh. Here comes Cicero.

Cicero My fellow-citizens –

Crowd (*cheers*)

Cicero I thank you for your applause but will you kindly reserve it. My

21

task today is a simple and also a happy one; I come before you to praise Pompey the Great.

Crowd   (*cheering*)

Cicero   Please, gentlemen! I stand here supporting a bill which, in case you have forgotten it, is not yet law. Though it will be law by this evening.

Crowd   (*cheers*)

Cicero   Those who oppose this bill – few though they be –

Crowd   (*some laughter*)

Cicero   Few though they be, they deserve, I think, an answer.

No less a man than Quintus Catulus has opposed this bill on the ground that it is a dangerous precedent. He seems to forget that this bill concerns only one man – Pompey; and Pompey's career has established many new precedents. But Pompey has never abused them. Catulus talks of revolution, but is Pompey a revolutionary?

Crowd   (*cries of 'No!'*)

Cicero   Of course not, my friends. Pompey is loyal to the core. The servant of the Senate and the People of Rome, he asks no more than to be their servant. Let him then serve you. Let him take over command of the war in the East and lead your legions to victory.

(*fade up Legionary march behind, then fade out*)

Crassus Gladiators, Caesar? That's a large sum for gladiators. Oh, I see, three hundred and twenty of 'em. And two more basilicas? Right, I'll settle the lot. The aedileship always incurs expense but you, my dear fellow, look like breaking the record. However. . . The people are with us, Caesar. If we can keep them with us till Pompey returns from the East and if only our friends to the left of us show a little self-control; if that fool Catiline, for instance, doesn't precipitate things –

(*sudden musical effect, giving the alarum*)

Informant Where's the consul? Where's Cicero?

Cicero   Here, my friend. I go to bed late these days. Well, have you got the evidence?

Informant Only too much, Cicero. Read this letter.

Cicero   Lentulus, Cethegus, Statilius. . . Five of them, I see, for Catiline.

Informant Two of them senators, Cicero.

Cicero   Yes, only two.

Informant You did not expect more?

Cicero   You know what I expected.

22

Informant Those other two gentlemen are clever. What will you do with the five?

Cicero Have them arrested at once. It will mean a debate in the Senate.

Informant You will not demand the death penalty?

Cicero Conspiracy is conspiracy. Catiline is out of Rome and those other two whose names begin with C are, as you say, clever. But the five birds that I have in my hands must die.

Informant It is a big decision.

Cicero I am consul. The first Cicero ever to enter the Senate.

Informant But there may be repercussions later. The people will support you now, of course, Catiline being their bogey-man, but once the crisis is over –

Cicero Yes, yes, I know. If only Pompey were here! But Cato at least will support me.

Informant Cato!

Cicero An honest man, a philosopher, but no diplomat.

Informant Cato! Cato's support can sometimes be a liability.

Crowd (*fade up murmuring of Senate House*)

Cato Fathers of the Senate! This city today is under martial law. And rightly so. Catiline is in Etruria under arms – a rebel. Five of his friends in Rome are, thanks to our noble consul, in prison – convicted traitors. These men count no longer as Rome citizens. Rome citizens? No! They are vermin – and you must kill them.

Crowd (*murmurs*)

Cato This being so, I am more than surprised, Senators, that one of your august number should have been found to plead for them. In the name, good God, of lenience. Were my great-grandfather alive –

Someone (*a laugh*)

Cato Laugh, fools, laugh; this, I see, is a tavern. Were, I repeat, Cato the Censor alive, he would have a word for such 'leniency.' And he would have a very black mark for a praetor elect, nay, more, for a man who has just become Pontifeux Maximus, if he dared to defend such traitors. Senators, I am appalled that you even listened to Caesar. He used, of course, many fine phrases – he always does – but why did he speak at all? I think he was trying to frighten you. He should be frightened himself. There are five men under arrest; there might have been more. Caesar may call for mercy; I doubt if he knows its meaning. I call out for justice – and I know that Cicero is with me. Let these five men die!

(*musical effect*)

23

Clodia Clodius, my darling brother!

Clodius Clodia, my darling sister! You great big ox-eyed Juno! What's the news from Baiae?

Clodia Oh, just some boring parties. All the real fun seems to happen these days in the Forum. Seen the praetor lately?

Clodius Which praetor? Oh you mean *the* praetor? My dear, I must tell you; I was around at the riot. Caesar versus Cato.

Clodia Yes, yes, I heard about that. A different story from last year. The Catiline business, you know. Extraordinary how Caesar's popular again. But with all that charm of course –

Clodius With all that technique, my dear. Just makes a sign with his hand and you should see the stones fly. Cato hadn't a chance. I can learn a lot from that man.

Clodia Cato, dear?

Clodius Witty, witty, witty! His wife has her points too.

Clodia Caesar's wife? I've never really noticed her.

Clodius Nor does he, very much. Still she has quite a nice figure.

Clodia Nice as mine?

Clodius Oh, vastly better than yours.

(*both laugh*)

Clodia No, my little tiny brother; I wouldn't, if I were you.

Clodius Wouldn't what?

Clodia Meddle with Caesar's wife. Not if you want him to help you up in the world.

Clodius Don't be silly, Clodia. Caesar will want *me*.

Clodia I can't see why he should.

Clodius Can't you? Pompey's just landed at Brindisi. After five years in the East. You know what that means?

Clodia 'The New Sulla.' But he just isn't a Sulla. He may have conquered the East and he may be a god to his legions but my bet is, when he hits Rome, he'll just be a damp squib. He's incurably law-abiding.

Clodius Have it your own way, Clodia. But, Pompey or no Pompey, Caesar will need me.

Clodia Caesar's wife won't. And you're quaestor elect, you nasty little boy. Why start off with a scandal?

Clodius Scandal! (*roars with laughter*) Clodia, are you yourself today? Or was it *you* I heard mention the word scandal? One would think, my darling, that you were a Vestal Virgin. Or at least some kind of virgin. Scandal! Well, well, scandal. . .

Woman   (female shriek)

  Maid This way! Hsh; they've seen you.

Women   (agitated babble of women)

  Maid Follow me quickly – cover your head with the hood. In here,
       Clodius! Quiet.

Women   (fade up babble of women)

Women's Voices (off) What! What! A man?

Aurelia (off) Close all the doors! There is a man in the house.

Women   A man! Where is he? Where is he?
           (fade out voices)

Clodius Now can I –

  Maid You can't get away yet. Don't raise your voice. They'll return.
       And for God's sake arrange your stola.

Clodius This female costume is really –

  Maid Why did you do it? I may be tortured for this.

Clodius Nonsense. I didn't come here for you.

  Maid I am aware of that. Who am I to compare with the wife of the
       Pontifex Maximus? After all I'm a slave.

Clodius A very nice little slave. Would Caesar sell you?

  Maid Keep your hands off me. Do you want me tortured?
           (Clodius sneezes)

  Maid Stop it!

Clodius How can I help it? It's all those damned burnt offerings.

  Maid A pretty time you chose to come seducing. Rites of the Bona Dea!
       It's unheard of – a man to come anywhere near them.

Clodius That is just what appealed to me.

  Maid But – but it's sacrilege.

Clodius Sacrilege (sneezes)

Aurelia (off) What's that? Come with me. Search that room in the
       corner.

  Maid Caesar's mother! . . . Oh, I shall be tortured.

Aurelia Come from behind that pillar! Who . . . are you? . . .
       You need not tell me. You are Publius Clodius.
           (musical effect and fade out)

Pompey My soldiers! After all these years you stand on Italian soil. Under
       my command you have conquered Pontus, Armenia, Cappa-
       docia, Paphlagonia, Media, Colchis, Albania, Syria, Cilicia, Meso-
       potamia. You have done in fact all that I asked of you. Today I
       thank you for it. For from today I am no longer your general.

Crowd   (murmur of surprise)

Pompey   I have called you here to dismiss you.

Crowd   (*shouts of 'No!' 'We protest!' etc.*)

Pompey   Silence! I have not dismissed you yet; I will have discipline. I will now, as is my custom, give you my reasons. In Rome at this moment they expect me to enter the city with my troops. They expect, that is, an unconstitutional action. They expect wrong, my friends. I believe in the constitution. You are the greatest army in the world; with men like you behind me I could emulate Sulla. I have no wish to do so. Your wars are over. You and I have shown ourselves good soldiers. Let us be now good citizens. And do not think for a moment that the State will be ungrateful. Far away there in the Forum under the Capital – you, my legions, you are the talk of Rome!

Crowd   (*fade up babble and behind*)

Voice   So Caesar divorced her at once? Quick work, eh?

Voice   'Above suspicion,' he said!

Voice   'Caesar's wife must be above suspicion!'

All   (*laughter*)

Voice   Caesar's wife! What about Caesar's mistresses?

All   (*laughter*)

Voice   It's a bit much all the same. It *was* a religious service.

Voice   That's right. You shouldn't mix love and religion.

Voice   The poor old goddess! What can *she* have thought?

All   (*laughter*)

Voice   Well, Clodius is for it anyway.

Voice   Ruin him, I should think.

Voice   I wonder.

Voice   Trial for sacrilege. Couldn't be worse.

Voice   No jury on earth would acquit him.

Voice   You think not? I wonder. . .

Clodia   Thank you, Marcus Crassus.

Crassus I think that should buy the jury. In spite of the fact that Cicero's going to bear witness and ruin your brother's alibi.

Clodia   Cicero! What's it to do with him? Why, Caesar himself has refused to give evidence.

Crassus Caesar is very forgiving – when it suits him.

Clodia   Cicero! I hate these self-made men. If he does come into court to refute that alibi – tell him to make his will first.

26

Crassus I'm not on such terms with him, Clodia. The only man he talks to these days is Pompey.

Clodia Very suitable, too. Mutual admiration by two back numbers. Can't you just hear them? 'When *I* defeated Mithradates.' 'When *I* saved the Republic.'

Cicero Yes, Pompey, when I saved the Republic – as the people phrased it at the time – I must tell you now that I often longed for your presence.

Pompey It would not seem to have been necessary.

Cicero Not to put down the conspiracy. No. That I could manage. But I was lonely, Pompey. I am the first of my family to enter the Senate – yet I've done more for the Senate than any man living. My colleagues were born old; they have no policy, Pompey. The nobility nowadays can't see beyond their fish-ponds. Take for example their attitude to yourself.

Pompey I do not understand it. Didn't I dismiss my legions?

Cicero We all respect you for *that*.

Pompey You may, Cicero. The Senate don't seem to. The least I expected was that they would ratify my actions. But you saw my reception in the House?

Cicero The Senate House, my dear friend, is a *milieu* that needs knowing.

Pompey I feel I have betrayed my soldiers. I promised them grants and –

Cicero Give me time. I will swing them round. You know my policy, Pompey. A solid front on the Right – the nobility and the financiers. If we can only hold these two upper classes together –

Pompey *If*, Cicero? *If!* The old guard in the Senate are – as you admit yourself – decadent, purblind, selfish. As for your bankers and other vested interests! They'll join whichever side pays. At the moment, it seems to me, they're veering over to the demagogues.

Cicero Crassus and Caesar, you mean? I don't believe it. Since my consulship they have both been discredited.

Pompey Caesar was quite successful as Praetor –

Cicero In an unconstitutional way.

Pompey Exactly; that was why he was successful. And now he's in Spain as propraetor with his pockets lined by Crassus and playing at being a soldier –

Cicero Yes, what do you think? Has he any military ability?

Pompey Not that I know of. Oh no doubt he'll be able to cope with the Spanish hill-tribes. But when a man's forty, as Caesar is now, he's past, I would think, learning the art of war. No, no, Cicero, Caesar as a soldier is negligible but Caesar as agitator –

Cicero Quite. And when he returns he's going to stand for consul.

Pompey And get elected probably –

Cicero Not if we stick together. You, Pompey, and I. And the Best People fall in behind us.

Pompey *If* they fall in behind us. And what when the mob falls in behind Crassus and Caesar?

Cicero The mob are about to learn a lesson. When their dear little playboy Clodius is convicted –

Pompey I don't understand that case. Why wouldn't Caesar give evidence?

Cicero Because he's *in* with Clodius; everyone knows that. But when, as I said, Clodius is convicted. . .

Gangster Clodius acquitted! Clodius acquitted! Now for the consular elections!

Crowd *(cheers)*
(Forum music and lose behind)

Catulus Citizens! I, Quintus Catulus, come before you today –

Voice Go home to bed!
(laughter)

Catulus I come before you today as an old man, but a patriot. I am not too old, however, to strike a blow for the right. You are assembled here to elect next year's consuls. It is a momentous occasion – one might call it a national emergency. There are two left-wing candidates, neither of whom can be trusted. Against them there is Bibulus –
(booing, hissing and lose behind)

Cato Citizens! If my great-grandfather –

Crowd *(rude laughter)*

Cato You know very well whom I mean. If he were here today he would vote for Bibulus. And remember that in our state the consuls are two, not one. Supposing that by ill fortune Caesar should be elected. Elect Bibulus too and all is well. For one consul can always veto the other. That is the constitution.

Clodius To hell with the constitution!
(uproar – from which emerges Caesar's fanfare)

28

Balbus But, my dear Cicero, you must be realistic. Why do you think Crassus supported Caesar?

Cicero For his own ends, I suppose. He has always hated the Senate.

Balbus Then why do you think Pompey supported Caesar?

Cicero That was an act of treachery. No, I won't mince my words; that was an act of treachery. And marrying Caesar's daughter! But it is Pompey's tragedy. A few months ago he belonged to our party; now he belongs nowhere.

Balbus Nonsense, Cicero. Pompey is not a traitor, merely a realist. Your dear friends of the Right let him down shamefully. Caesar, now he is consul, will make amends for that. But why can't you, my dear Cicero, show yourself a realist? The door's still open. That's why Caesar sent me here. In Rome today there are only three men that count; you can still make a fourth with them.

Cicero A fourth with whom, Balbus? With a declassé demagogue, a crook millionaire and a renegade!

Balbus I shall tell him then that you decline? Perhaps I should remind you that Clodius, who is not exactly a friend of yours – Clodius wants to be tribune.

Cicero Clodius is not qualified for the tribuneship.

Balbus Caesar could make him qualified.

Cicero Bibulus will stop that.

Balbus *Who* will stop that?

Cicero Our ancestors, Balbus, were wise to invent the dual consulship. Two men to check each other. When Pompey and Crassus were consuls, the Right was unrepresented. This is totally different. We can depend on Bibulus.

Balbus I have no doubt you can.

Cicero We can. From New Year's Day, when both of them enter their consulship –

Balbus I suppose he'll hear thunder on the left.

(*up thunder – orchestral – and out*)

Bibulus Fathers of the Senate! I veto this bill.

(*drown in thunder*)

Clodius Stand by, boys. I want you all with me today in the popular Assembly. Caesar is taking his bill to the people.

Crowd (*cries of 'Good!'*)

Clodius And all his other bills after it. No more talkie-talkie up there in the Senate House. The people must speak for themselves – and you must help 'em. So all of you be there on time. Ex-gladiators near

29

the platform; the rest of you in groups as usual on the outskirts. And if any of you runs into Bibulus – or Cato – or my old friend Cicero –

Crowd   (laughter)

Clodius   Give him my salutations. You know how.

        (laughter and cross-fade into short snatch of Forum music)

Official Voice   Julian Law, passed today in the Assembly –

Pompey   Thank God for that; at least he's kept his promise. I'd rather it had been done in a more legal manner but . . . beggars can't be choosers. I have to think of my veterans.

Official Voice   Julian Law, passed today in the Assembly –

Crassus   At long last. My friends the tax-farmers ought to be happy now. Contracts for two-thirds the price.

Official Voice   Julian Law, passed today in the Assembly –

Cisalpine   There! What did I tell you? You remember long ago when he came by here from Spain? I told him then that we provincials trusted him. No more official extortion in the provinces.

Official Voice   Julian Law, passed today in the Assembly –

Clodius   Well, my dear sister, I am no longer your brother. By Caesar's new law I've become an adopted plebeian. So now I can stand for the tribuneship. Then look out for thunder.

        (orchestral thunder)

Cato   Thunder on the left. All these proceedings are illegal.

        (thunder)

Bibulus   I am observing the heavens. All Caesar's acts are illegal.

        (thunder)

Joker   Consulship of Caesar and Bibulus? Ha! Consulship of Julius and Caesar!

Cicero   But where is it going to end? And now that Pompey's his son-in-law –

        (fade up babble of Senate House)

Pompey   Fathers of the Senate! As Gaius Julius Caesar is due to retire from his consulship – an office which he has held with such distinction –

        (cries of 'Hear! Hear!', 'Question!' 'Shame!')

I rise to renew the question of his ensuing command. You have already appointed him to a governorship – that of Cisalpine Gaul.

        (slight laughter)

The province of Cisalpine Gaul is in itself peaceful. It is, however, at this moment threatened from beyond the Alps. If then you confine Caesar to the southern side of the Alps, you confine him to the defensive. I speak as a soldier, gentlemen.

Crowd (*'Hear! Hear!'*)

Pompey I propose therefore an amendment. Give Caesar a command on *both* sides of the Alps – with the necessary staff and such troops as he may require – and insure him in this command for a five-year term.

Cato Five years! Why so long?

Pompey You cannot defeat the Gauls in a day, Cato; I speak as a soldier. Why, it took me nearly as long to dispose of the war in the East.

Cato That was a very bad precedent!

Pompey I object to that remark.

Crowd (*cries of 'Withdraw! Withdraw!'*)

Cato I never withdraw what is true.

Pompey Senators! Leave Cato alone – for so he always has been – and let me put my motion. First let me recapitulate –

Cato One last word before that! If you vote for this motion of Pompey's you know what you vote for? A tyranny, Senators, a tyranny! Give Caesar those provinces and legions – and you might as well cut your throats. I know the man, I tell you. The moment he dons the scarlet cloak of a general, the moment the first reveille sounds in his camp –

  (*fade up trumpet in distance*)

Then the Republic is doomed!

  (*up trumpet – Caesar's fanfare – and to close*)

Clodia Yes, darling. I like your poem a lot.

  'Who goeth now the darkling journey
    From which, we are told, is no returning.'

But I can't really remember that I felt like that about my sparrow. I have such lots of little birds and they're always dying, you see. Oh don't look like that, Catullus! What have I said now? Cage-birds are all very well but today I've got other things to think about. My brother Clodius – you know why he became tribune? To settle accounts with Cicero. Well, now he's about to do it. He's digging up Cicero's action in putting those people to death, the Catiline business, remember? So if the old fool – oh your face! I forgot you liked that windbag. If the old fool has any sense he'll pack up and leave Rome tonight. Oh don't look at me like that! Come and kiss me, Catullus. You know I adore you, darling.

Cicero Take this letter; I would write it myself, only my hand is shaking.

'Cicero to Atticus, greeting. You ask me not to think of suicide – but tell me what I have to live for. Clodius has had me outlawed. That Caesar was behind Clodius you know as well as I do. What I cannot forgive is Pompey's lack of courage. He refused to intervene on the grounds that Clodius was a tribune. And he, Pompey, merely a private citizen! But soon, I think, he may repent it. They tell me that Clodius, like a mad dog who must always be biting someone, is now transferring his attentions – ' What's wrong with that light, Xanthias?

Xanthias I'm sorry master. We have no more oil.

Cicero No more oil? No. . . That does not surprise me either.

    (*fade up chanting*)

Gang Pompey the Great was always late!

    Who – wants – Pompey?

    Pompey the Great –

Clodius No, no, no! Pompey the Big now.

Gang Pompey the Big is a –

Clodius No! From the beginning again.

Gang Pompey the Great was always late!

    Who – wants – Pompey?

    Pompey the Big is a stuck-up pig!

    Into the ditch with Pompey!

Clodius Fine. Now you know where he lives? Be there at dawn tomorrow – he comes to the Forum early – and say your piece as he appears. With love from Clodius, boys. I'll teach him who rules Rome.

    (*gang repeats chant; fade out*)

Centurion Come here, you! Yes, you. The other recruits dismiss. Off with you to your porridge. That's what you're going to conquer Gaul on.

    Now then, son. You come from Rome, don't you?

Recruit Yes, I –

Centurion Stand up straight. You're in the army now. Caesar's army at that. Know what that means, pale-face?

Recruit Yes, I –

Centurion I'll tell you what it means. See those piles over there along the rampart – each of 'em looks like an ironmonger's shop? Well, one of those piles is yours, chum. That's what you're going to carry for twenty miles per day. Sword, shield, two seven-foot javelins, two or three stakes on your left shoulder, helmet round your waist, fortnight's grain rations, cooking-pot, mug, saw, basket, hatchet, sickle, pick, spade. And you know what you do when you've finished your twenty miles?

Recruit Well, I suppose I –

Centurion Shut up! When a centurion asks a recruit a question, he don't expect no answer. When you've marched your twenty miles through Gaul, you buckle to and you *dig*. Dig, I said. With that spade. And if you can't dig, you're no damn use to Caesar. There never was such a bloody man for digging. I've served my time under Pompey, so I should know. Pompey? Can't see *him* as a civilian. *He* always stood on his dignity.

(fade up gang-chant, peak and fade out)

Pompey There's nothing for it. I must write to Caesar. If I had two platoons I could deal with Clodius, but as it is – How can a private citizen live in this city? Why did I ever let them banish Cicero?

(fade up snatch of Caesar's fanfare and out)

Cicero Fathers of the Senate! When I returned from exile last year my first public act was to propose a public thanksgiving for Caesar's victories in Gaul. This fact alone should make clear that the measure I am now about to propose is in no way tinctured with, much less motivated by, any hostility to Caesar.

When therefore I, Marcus Tullius Cicero, recommend to you the temporary suspension of one of the laws which Caesar passed as consul, I mean his agrarian law disposing of land in Campania. . .

(exclamations. Cross-fade into Caesar's fanfare)

Agent Caesar! Here is the report you asked for; Cicero's speech in full. You will find it confirms your suspicions. It is the first blow in an attack on your policy as consul. It also seems to be intended to estrange yourself and Pompey. Pompey, of course, is already estranged from Crassus. So I take it the conference is on? Right. I will let the parties know. Lucca you said, I think? Right, Caesar. I'll arrange it.

Cisalpine Well now, isn't this a great day for Lucca? I always knew that Caesar would come to the top – but not to a top like this. Did you see Crassus when he passed? Did you see Pompey? They looked a bit awkward, didn't they? The Three Big Men they call them but every triangle has an apex. And I know who the apex is this time.

33

B

(Caesar's fanfare)

Crassus Well, my dear Pompey? So, after fifteen years, we shall be colleagues again.

Pompey Crassus! You seem unwontedly gay this evening. I suppose it's the prospect of your command in Syria.

Crassus That is the year after next.

Pompey Quite so – but that's what you're thinking of. Let me tell you, Crassus; it's some time, I think, since you've been in the field. A large-scale war is not – to use a phrase you'll understand – really a safe investment.

Crassus Your father-in-law and yourself have done quite well from such wars.

Pompey Why will you call him my father-in-law?

Crassus But he is.

Pompey Of course he is – but I'm fifty, Caesar may be bald but he's younger than I am. Do you want to make me ridiculous?

Crassus Want to? No. Why should I?

Pompey It *has* gone to your head. All right. Keep your illusions. The year after next you go out and defeat the Parthians. Who've never yet been defeated. But in the meantime you're to be consul with me. I trust you will fill that office like a gentleman.

Crassus Didn't you find me a gentleman last time, Pompey? Come, come, come, why are you getting so heated? This conference here at Lucca has been on the whole satisfactory. You've got what you want, I've – er – got what I want; all that remains now is to square Cicero.

Pompey I have undertaken to do that. As soon as I am back in Rome, Cicero will make a speech. Recanting his recent uncalled-for attack on Caesar. And – more positively – speaking in support of the motion that Caesar's command in Gaul be extended for five more years.

Crassus That should make him popular with the conservatives!

Pompey Popular? Poor Cicero!

(snatch of Forum music)

Cato Five more years! Cicero! You are a renegade.

(snatch of Forum music)

Cicero Continue my letter, please. 'The better of our two consuls – and I still admire Pompey though some would attribute such a statement to hypocrisy – has just treated the public to an astonishing spectacle. The elephants were reserved till the last day and certainly impressed the crowd – without apparently pleasing them; their cries as they died struck me as almost human. But the smell of the circus is less than the smell of dictatorship and I shed no tears any more either for beast or man; is not our whole state dying?'

(*funeral music, stronger, then down to background*)

Centurion Get on there! Kill 'em! Yours not to reason why. Caesar's orders, I tell you.

Yes, men, women, and children. Don't leave one of 'em. I know it's not nice. It's your job. Caesar knows best. Kill 'em.

(*up music and fade out slowly*)

Cato Fathers of the Senate! I rise to accuse Caesar. You have heard the news from Gaul. Caesar concluded a peace, in your name and in mine, with two Germanic tribes. And after concluding that peace, Caesar murdered those tribes. Men, women, and children. The number concerned, according to his own account, is four hundred and thirty thousand. I therefore hereby give notice that, so soon as Caesar's command in Gaul expires, I shall indict him for this. That is all I need say now.

(*fade up funeral music and to background*)

Drunk Well, who's dead now? Caesar's daughter, d'ye say? And who's Caesar's daughter? Oh, Pompey's wife? And who's Pompey's wife? Oh, Caesar's daughter? I see.

(*fade out music*)

Cicero There goes a link between them. The strongest perhaps. I must send my condolences to Pompey. Xanthias, my writing tablets! There is still a balance of power, there is still Crassus. Once he's defeated the Parthians –

(*fade up barbaric percussion and behind*)

Crassus Gentlemen, this is the end. For two days we have retreated through the desert. We have been cut to pieces. Pompey was right – damn him – when he warned me against the Parthians.

Now, as you see, the Parthian emissary has called me to go to a conference. I know what that means; these people's treachery is only equalled by their horsemanship. But I call you to witness, gentlemen. I am not Pompey or Caesar; I remain Crassus. Yet history would rather record that I was deceived by the Parthian than abandoned by my own legions. Goodbye. I go to this 'conference'.

(*bring up percussion to climax and clean out*)

35

Cicero So much for the balance of power. Now there are only two.

Milo Cicero! Cicero!

Cicero Come in, Milo my friend. What brings you here before dawn?

Milo What do you think?

Cicero Yes. It is terrible news. Crassus is dead. All the more reason that you should stand for consul.

Milo I fully intend to stand for consul. In spite of the message thrown in at my window by Clodius yesterday.

Cicero What did the message say?

Milo 'If you stand for consul you are as good as dead.' But I replied of course. Two of my men picked up a stray Clodian. Took up his corpse and left it on Clodius' doorstep. Strip of papyrus stuck in his back with a dagger. Message on it in blood: 'I have gladiators too.'

Well? You look shocked.

Cicero I am shocked to think that a man like you, Milo, can only deal with Clodius by imitating his methods.

Milo Imitating? I go one better than Clodius. And why be shocked. *You* couldn't deal with him, could you?

Cicero No. You are probably right. Would you like to read this? Electioneering suggestions. Nicely phrased, I think.

Milo I'm sure it is, my dear Cicero. But nice phrases alone won't win me *this* election.

(*fade up riot music, peak and to background*)

Birria! Where did you stab him?

Birria Only in the shoulder, Milo. Sorry. He ducked too quick.

Milo Then he'll still be alive in that tavern they got him to?

Birria Oh yes, he'll be alive. I know that pansy type. They die a lot harder than you'd think.

Milo Well, I don't want Clodius alive. Birria, round up the others, break your way into that tavern – and this time make a job of it.

Birria Just as you say, Milo.

(*peak music, mix with cries of 'Fire' and out*)

Pompey Fathers of the Senate! I accept the heavy burden you lay upon me. Yesterday Clodius was killed and within a few hours his followers had burnt our Senate House. Today Rome is in panic. The consular elections are still postponed and the radicals are impeaching Milo for murder.

(*cry of 'Shame'*)

Unjustly, as we agree.

36

('*hear! hear!*')

This being so I accept – for the time being – the extraordinary office you press on me, the office of sole consul. I accept it, gentlemen, not for my sake but for yours. And I undertake to keep order throughout the city.

The mob may have burnt the Senate House; they shall never destroy the Senate.

And it goes without saying that Milo shall get a fair trial. Cicero, as you know, will be counsel for the defence. *I* shall keep order in the court.

(*cheering and fade out*)

Milo Take a letter, my dear boy. Milo to Cicero, greeting. The weather in Marseilles is good, I am having the time of my life. Thank you for sending me the speech you would have delivered if Pompey had really kept order and you had not lost your nerve. But I don't reproach you of course. If I hadn't been convicted for murder, I shouldn't be here in Marseilles sampling these excellent mullet. Look after your health, my dear Cicero.

(*fade up Caesar's fanfare and out*)

Centurion Well, well, well, what goings on in the world. These last few years I've thought Gaul was hot enough but from what I hear of Rome . . . ! High time Baldy went back there and settled it. And all of us here are behind him if it comes to a fight. Not that I want to fight my old chief Pompey but if he lines up with the Senate and that's what they say he's doing –

Cicero You must be firm, Pompey. I've often asked you before to take the place that belongs to you. As leader of the Conservatives. Though now it may be too late.

Pompey I tell you Cicero: if I but stamp my foot –

Cato I've never asked you for anything in my life. I used to distrust you, Pompey. But I ask you now, in the name of our ancient Roman virtues, come in with us quickly – and act!

Pompey But Caesar's not yet technically in rebellion. He's still negotiating. So are you.

Cato Yes, and you know his demands?

We can see what Caesar wants and our answer to him is No!

Pompey But that may mean civil war.

Cato We cannot appease Caesar. Let the Senate negotiate if it salves their conscience; it will all come to nothing.

(*fade up March of the Legions and build behind*)

Voice Negotiations . . .

Voice Negotiations . . .

Voice Negotiations . . .

Voice Negotiations . . .

Voice Negotiations . . .

Music (*orchestra out and drumroll alone behind*)

Centurion So this is the Rubicon? Why, it's only a brook.

(*drumroll into fanfare and add orchestra for climax*)

Cato Fathers of the Senate! Many of you, I see, have appeared today in mourning. If you had listened to me, Cato, during these last ten years, you would not need black robes now. However, you did not listen. Caesar has crossed the Rubicon. That is that. I do not believe in relying on a single man but, as things are, we have to. Only Pompey is a match for Caesar. Right. Let us waste no time. Senators, we are at war. Let Pompey conduct it.

(*fade up march and to close*)

Pothinus So Pompey is coming to Egypt.

Theodotus Yes. Defeated.

Pothinus He will expect a reception?

Theodotus Of course. What kind would be fitting? Speak first, Pothinus; you are the King's eunuch.

Pothinus Ah, but you're a professor. You speak first, Theodotus.

Theodotus Well, in my humble opinion, this is a simple case. In the debating school I would only give it to beginners. Pompey has been badly defeated by Caesar but he has forces elsewhere – Cato, they say, is in Africa. Yet the odds are that Caesar will win. So, if we receive Pompey, we shall have Caesar our enemy. But if we reject Pompey, Pompey will hate us – and then what will happen supposing he wins after all. Ergo, one course remains: lure him on shore and kill him. Caesar will be very grateful and Pompey cannot retaliate. Q.E.D. Dead men do not bite.

Wife Wait, Pompey, wait! You can't go ashore in that!

Pompey Cornelia, my wife, why not? That is what they have sent for me.

Wife A dinghy! But it's an insult.

Pompey It is in proportion to my fortune.

Wife But I don't like the looks of those men,

Pompey Egyptians, only Egyptians.

Wife Pompey, I'm scared. Don't go!

38

Pompey It is too late to be scared. Pull in there, fellows, pull alongside!

Wife I knew it. Look at their faces. You're walking into a trap.

Pompey With Egyptian galleys all round us, Cornelia dear, if it's a trap, there's no way of avoiding it. But if it *is* a trap, then I *shall* walk into it. Upright.

Goodbye, Cornelia. I may lose my life now – and lose you too. Losses follow each other, it would seem. Till I met Caesar at Pharsalus I never lost a battle. But it's no good dwelling on that. All right, Egypt, I'm coming!

Just before I go, your hood. There. Over your eyes. Goodbye, Cornelia, and go back to Rome when you can. Caesar will treat you well.

(*fade up high note and hold behind*)

Theodotus There you are, gentlemen. Q.E.D.

(*note into chord and out*)

Cicero So Pompey is dead. The old order is finished. The sun has fallen from the sky and yet I, Cicero, live. I will make my peace with Caesar. And that leaves only Cato. I suppose it's no good hoping that *he* will make his peace.

(*fade up Caesar's fanfare, hold at peak and out*)

Cato That trumpet sounds very near. Is it Caesar's?

Son I heard no trumpet, Father – but Caesar's certainly approaching. You had better leave Utica quickly. As your men did.

Cato My men betrayed their cause.

Son The people of Utica, Father, intend to betray *you*.

Cato I know they do. I shall not give them the chance. Am I not descended from Cato the Censor? Leave me alone now, son, sleep well – for so shall I. Goodnight, my son. God bless you.

Son Goodnight, Father.

Cato Come back! Come back!

Son Yes, Father?

Cato Has anyone taken my sword?

Son No, Father, of course not.

Cato It was hanging at the head of my bed. I am your father and I am still a commander. Hand me that book of Plato's. Thank you, son. Now bring me back my sword.

Son Yes, Father.

Cato Plato on Immortality: 'A man who has spent his life in philosophy will naturally meet his death with – '

Slave (*approach*) Pardon, please, pardon. Your son sent this.

39

Cato   Thank you. Is the edge keen? Yes. Now, I am master of myself. Yes, Caesar may be master of the world but I am a Stoic, I am master of myself. A keen edge. Good. Let Caesar have his triumph!
(fade up song of the Legionaries and down to background)

2nd Freedwoman   What a procession! It's the best triumph I've seen.
(up song and to background)

Cicero   Altars blazing, statues wreathed with flowers, trumpets, tableaux, sacrificial oxen. And captives – from years back – paraded once, then killed. And that figure there in the chariot crowned with laurel. At this distance it might be Pompey. No! I must go home.
(fade out song)

Voice   Heard what they say? That Egyptian princess what's her name – Cleopatra – is living over there in a villa beyond the Tiber?

Voice   Very good measure of his, reforming the Senate.

Voice   Yes – and reforming the calendar.

Voice   Yes – but what about his head on the coinage?

Voice   And what about his image being placed among the gods?

Voice   And this lifetime dictatorship? There's never been such a thing.

Voice   Yes, and have you read his book against Cato! Scandalous!

Voice   Yes, yes, yes – but he's codifying the laws.

Voice   And he's got great schemes for the provinces.

Voice   Yes – and for draining the Pontine marshes.

Voice   Oh, he's a statesman all right.

Voice   Statesman? That's not my name for it.

Cicero   *(yawning)* Writing tablets? Where are my writing tablets? Xanthias!

Xanthias   Yes, sir.

Cicero   Writing – No, I don't want them. I think I'll take my siesta. That's one thing I'm grateful to Caesar for.

Xanthias   What, sir?

Cicero   Before his time, when men were allowed to talk politics, I was kept terribly busy; I had no time for siestas.

Xanthias   Do you want anything else, sir?

Cicero   Yes, fill up that water-clock. Time's running out again. See?

Xanthias   Yes, sir. Time is like that. Always later than you think, sir.

Schoolmaster   Good Lord, boys, see the time? It's always later than you think. The school bell will go in a moment, and we haven't finished with Caesar. Not that one ever does.

40

No bell yet? The clock must be fast; let's get to the Ides of March. You've read about that in Shakespeare. Two shadows that look very tall but perhaps they weren't really. Names of Brutus and Cassius. And the Ides of March remember, was always a kind of Bank Holiday. Fun and games in the Campus Martius.

(*fade up holiday music behind*)

Caesar was late going down to the Senate that morning, the common folk in the Campus must all have been tiddly by then. The day was sacred to a goddess called Anna Perenna, an old Italian goddess, a wee bit rustic. She seems to have filled the role of a patron saint of the year. For the year, remember, boys, began in March. Glorious weather probably. Think of it, boys, think of it. The Ides of March are come!

(*up holiday music, then lose behind*)

2nd Freedwoman Drink up, old soldier. Drink yourself longer life.

Centurion I've had twenty-one cups already. That means twenty-one years. Well, twenty-one years from now I think I'll be old enough. Damn it, woman, I'm an ex-Serviceman: first a veteran of Pompey's – it was Pompey made me centurion, let us respect his memory –

2nd Freedwoman Let us respect his memory.

Centurion And then under Caesar – the gods preserve him –

2nd Freedwoman The gods preserve him!

Centurion Ten years in Gaul in the Tenth Legion. Long live the Tenth Legion!

2nd Freedwoman Long live the Tenth Legion!

Centurion And three years after that in those bloody civil wars – I was at Pharsalus, did I ever tell you?

2nd Freedwoman Yes, yes, you did ever tell me.

Centurion *Yes*, I was at Pharsalus. Well, what was I talking about? Oh yes; add up all that and twenty-one years on top of it and I'll be old enough. So I won't drink no more.

2nd Freedwoman Oh yes you will! You've only drunk for yourself. Now you can drink for Caesar.

Centurion All right. Drink for Caesar.

2nd Freedwoman Just a moment. How old's Caesar now? Late fifties, isn't he?

Centurion What?

2nd Freedwoman Yes, late fifties. Right. Here we begin. 'I pray for as many more years of life for Caesar as I can drink cups of wine.' Here, here, take the cup.

Centurion I pray for as many –
(groan and crash)
2nd Freedwoman Hey! Hey! What's wrong with you?
Passed out?
Passed out cold.
(up finale and through)

East of the Sun and West of the Moon

A Norwegian Folk Tale

First broadcast in the BBC Third Programme on 25 July 1959 in Louis MacNeice's production, with music by Tristram Cary and the following cast:

HELGA	*Beth Boyd*
FATHER	*James Thomason*
HALVOR	*Patricia Hayes*
MOTHER	*Betty Hardy*
PRINCE	*Jeremy Spenser*
CRONES	*Patience Collier*
EAST WIND AND PARROT	*Garard Green*
WEST WIND	*Liam Gaffney*
SOUTH WIND	*Dino Galvani*
NORTH WIND	*Laidman Browne*

.

Singer East of the sun and west of the moon –
          Fear at midnight, fear at noon –
          Stands a castle all men shun
          West of the moon and east of the sun.

          West of the moon and east of the sun,
          Hopes unwoven, joys undone,
          Falls the darkness late and soon
          East of the sun and west of the moon.

          East of the sun and west of the moon
          Shows no mercy, grants no boon;
          All loves wither one by one
          West of the moon and east of the sun.

          West of the moon and east of the sun
          White ghosts walk and dark shades run.
          Dine with the devil – but use your spoon
          East of the sun and west of the moon.
              (*a shivering chord*)

Helga Father! What was that?
Father The wind, Helga; the wind in the pine trees.
Halvor It wasn't. It was a troll.
Mother Halvor! I've told you before. There are no trolls in this valley. A
          power of shadow and mist, but trolls? Definitely not.
Halvor Oh yes there are; I've seen 'em. With great long curly claws and
          great long dripping noses. And I've seen werewolves too and swan-
          maidens and St Peter.
Mother Halvor, you'll go to bed at once. Without your supper.
Halvor There isn't any supper.
Father That's true.
Mother And *you* can hold your tongue. Whose fault is it there isn't a crust
          in the house? Call yourself a woodcutter! When did you last fell a
          tree, even a wee one?
Father How can I use an axe when my arm's broken?
Mother You broke it when you were drunk; you broke it on purpose.
Halvor It was a troll did it. He tripped up father by the heels and . . .

45

Mother Halvor!
> (*slap and wail*)

Helga Oh mother!

Mother Helga, I'll slap you too if . . .

Father Be quiet. Come here Halvor.

Mother You'll spoil that child. Just as you've spoiled Helga. Always looking in the looking-glass when she ought to be spinning or scrubbing. You don't catch me looking in the glass.

Father (*aside*) Just as well for the glass.

Mother What's that?

Father Nothing.

Mother If Helga's not going to work, she'd better clear out and get married.

Helga How can I, mother? All the young men in this valley have gone far away to the towns.

Father And I don't blame them. They fancy a glimpse of the sun.

Mother *You* don't blame them! When I married you, Thorstein, I expected to live in the city in a decent house, with servants, like your parents lived in. If I'd ever dreamed that, for all your grand education, we'd end up here in this valley. . .

Father Who says we've ended up? When my arm's mended, do you know what I'm going to do? Cut down one more tree – only one, but a choice one – then take my chisel and my jack-knife and carve things.

Mother What things?

Father Carvings. Beautiful figures. Birds, bears, goats, little ships, the ancient vikings our ancestors . . . Saints and bishops . . . shepherds . . . girls with breasts.

Mother Disgusting!

Father Then I'll go down to the towns and everyone will clamour to buy them.

Helga Father, how lovely! I never knew you were a carver.

Mother He's not. Go on, contradict me.
> (*pause*)

Halvor Go on father, contradict her.

Father I can't. It was only a dream. I have no talent for carving.

Helga Then we'll always be poor?

Father Yes, Helga. Poor till we die.
> (*three taps on door*)

Mother What's that?

Halvor It's a troll.

46

(slap and short wail)

Father It's the wind.

(three taps again)

Mother That door needs fixing. As soon as your arm's mended. . .

(three taps again)

Helga It can't be the wind. The wind's never so regular.

Father I'll have a look.

Mother Easy now, opening that door. We don't want the snow blowing in.

(opening of rough door)

Helga A bear!

Halvor Don't let him eat me!

Father He won't; can't you see he's a white bear? Come in sir.

(closing of door)

Bear Gf! Good evening all.

Father Anything I can do for you?

Bear Gf! Yes. Do you want to be rich?

Mother Don't ask daft questions.

Bear Gf! I can make you as rich as you now are poor. But on one condition.

Father What's that?

Bear Gf! You must give me your daughter.

Helga Oh no, no, no!

Mother Don't interrupt, Helga. You were complaining just now how there's no young men in this valley –

Helga But a bear, mother! I'd rather die an old maid.

Father I'm sorry, sir, it's very kind of you, but if my daughter is not so disposed –

Mother Not so disposed? I'll dispose her! Listen, mister. When you say rich, exactly how rich do you mean?

Bear I will give you a house as large as you want and as many servants as you want and tapestries on all the walls and swansdown beds in the bedrooms and for Sundays a dinner service of gold –

Mother What about weekdays?

Bear Gf! Another for weekdays.

Mother In that case –

Helga No, mother, stop it! I've said no and I mean no. That bear may be as white as snow but look at his size and his jaws and his paws –

Mother Ssh! Don't take offence mister. You just come back here next Thursday. She'll have changed her tune by then maybe.

47

    Bear Gf! Thank you. Next Thursday then. Goodnight everyone. Gf!
          (*door opens and shuts*)

    Helga Never, never, never, never! Father supports me anyway. Don't
          you father?
          (*pause*)

    Father Well, 'm. . .

    Halvor I like that bear. He has nice eyes.

    Mother He has a nice proposition.

    Father Well, we have a week to talk it over.

    Helga Father! You're not going to –

    Father Nice eyes and, for a bear, nice manners. Besides, he didn't say he
          wanted to marry you.

    Helga But that's worse!

    Father I don't mean that either.

    Helga But what else would he want me for?

    Father Well, 'm, people keep bears just as pets –

    Helga In cages.

    Father And some people train them to dance. That might be it. As men
          keep dancing bears, so bears might keep dancing girls.

    Helga But I've never learnt to dance.

    Mother You can start learning now. Thorstein, where's your old
          fiddle?

    Halvor Here it is, on the peg. Here you are father.

    Mother We'd best begin with an easy one. Try the 'Dance of the blue billy-
          goat'.
          (*fiddle begins and behind*)

    Father Is that it?

    Mother That's it. Now, Helga, up on your feet lass, and do exactly what I
          do.
          (*fiddle*)

    Father Come on Helga. Follow your mother.

    Helga Well, if I must –

    Mother One moment. Thorstein!
          (*fiddle breaks off*)

    Father What is it? I was playing it right.

    Mother That's just it. How do you come to be playing it at all? With that
          famous broken arm of yours!
          (*pause*)
          Aye, I might have known. You've been fooling me. Too idle to
          go back to the woodcutting. All right then, you can pay for it. If

you won't chop trees, you can fiddle – fiddle from now to next Thursday.

(*fiddle and fade out – then fade up again, new tune*)

One – two – three, etc.

(*three loud knocks on door*)

(*fiddle breaks off*)

Father Come in.

(*door opens and shuts*)

Bear Gf! Good evening. Has she changed her mind?

Mother Aye certainly.

Helga No!

Mother Helga, here's your bundle. How can you say 'no' when you just packed it yourself!

Helga Yes, but now I see him again . . . looming so big with his paws and his jaws –

Bear And my eyes? Helga, look in my eyes.

(*pause*)

Do I frighten you still?

Helga No. How strange.

Bear Then we'll be off to where I live. It's a long way but you can ride on my back. And, Thorstein, the moment we pass through this door, you'll be free of this valley for ever – no more swirling mist or leaks in the roof or ghosts of food in the larder or ghosts of your youth in the trees. From now on you'll live in a mansion.

Mother Not a castle?

Bear Oh very well; a castle.

Helga Goodbye father . . . mother. . . Goodbye my dearest Halvor.

All Goodbye Helga.

(*door opens and closes – transformation effect*)

Halvor Ooh, what a big, big room! And look at all the rooms beyond it!

Father Ha! ha! ha! ha! ha!

Mother What's wrong with you?

Father Your head! On the top of your head!

Mother What's on the top of – St Olaf of the Rocks! A tiara!

Father And a velvet gown! And I'm in velvet too!

Halvor And I'm in velvet too.

Mother Well, mind you don't go spilling egg on it. St Brynhild of the Goose-Quills! What's this in my hand? An inventory!

Father Well, that bear is certainly business-like. If he's as kind as he's efficient, well, perhaps poor Helga'll be all right with him after all.

49

(fade up padding of bear)
(padding comes to a stop)

Helga   What a long ride: I hope I'm not too heavy for you!

Bear   Gf! We're there.

Helga   Where?

Bear   Home.

Helga   But it's just a rocky hill.

Bear   Gf! You watch. We knock on this rock and –

    (knocking and rock doors opening)

Helga   Oh I'm dazzled. All these lights – and their reflections!

Bear   Gf! I need them. I have no windows, you see.

Helga   It's like church on Christmas Eve – but lots of churches one after each other. How many rooms have you got?

Bear   Gf! I've never counted. Never been into half of them.

Helga   But the gold and the silver! You must be the richest bear in Norway.

Bear   Gf! Richest bear in the world.

Helga   Oh!

Bear   What is it now?

Helga   Myself in that great long mirror. And there I am again – and again – and again! And every time in that long white dress. Is it true?

Bear   Gf! Feel it and see.

Helga   But how soft it is! What is this stuff called?

Bear   Silk.

Helga   So this is what silk is.

Bear   Gf! Come into the dining-room.

    (footsteps of bear and Helga – and to a stop)

Bear   Gf! I expect you're hungry after that ride on my back. Well, the table's all laid, as you see –

Helga   But it's only laid for one.

Bear   Here's a silver bell. Ring it for anything you want.

Helga   And servants will come?

Bear   Whatever you want will come.

Helga   But surely –

Bear   Gf! I can't be bothered with servants. And now, Helga, I must leave you –

Helga   But I'll be all alone here. At the head of a table the length of a ship and only my own reflection over and over and over –

Bear   Goodnight Helga. Eat well and sleep well. Gf!

Helga Goodnight. (*pause*) Come on, Helga, be brave. Try if this silver
bell works. First – let's see – a nice bowl of bilberry soup.
(*tinkle of echoing bell*)
St Hrolf the Victualler! And in a golden bowl! 'm, delicious.
What about bread? White bread!
(*tinkle of bell*)
And *how* white it is! If mother could see me now – not only drinking soup from a golden bowl, but eating real white bread, as white
as snow, as white as the white bear. . .

Mother If only our poor Helga could see us now! With all those liveried
servants standing there at attention –
Father Those dummies take away my appetite.
Mother Rubbish!
Halvor They don't take away mine – Can I have some more mutton?
Mother Lamb, Halvor, lamb. No, you can't.
Halvor Then can I have more red jelly?
Mother No, you ought to be in bed.
Halvor Bed! On our first night here!
Father Bed? First night? Poor Helga. I wonder what's going to happen
to her.
(*tinkle of silver bell*)
Helga Oh! These sheets, these pillows – why, these must be silk too. And
this great brocaded canopy! But this bed is so big I'll be lost in it.
And I'm so sleepy, the trouble of undressing – if only there were
someone to undress me! Someone? Helga, don't be silly; here we
don't bother with servants. Let me be naked and in bed please.
(*tinkle of bell*)
An ocean of swansdown – sinking – sinking – but how do I put
out the light? Oh, of course; the bell again.
(*tinkle of bell*)
There! Dark as black velvet. And now to sleep, to sleep. (*yawns*)
Come on, girl, shut your eyes. Yes, but there's a gap in my eye-
lids – gap in the dry stone wall – gap in my past, my future.
Something coming through it, something white. Of course!
Those are what one counts. Sheep . . . white lambs . . . bears. One
sheep, two sheep, three sheep; one lamb, two lambs, three lambs,
four – no, he's black leave him out of it; four lambs, five lambs,
six lambs. And now for the bears: one bear –

Prince One bear's enough, Helga.
Helga Who're you? You're not a bear.
Prince Do I feel like one?
Helga No . . . no, you feel like a dream.
Prince Perhaps that's how you'd better think of me. Closer, Helga dear, closer.
Helga Like that? But should I be doing this?
Prince Of course you should. You're dreaming.
Helga Yes, only dreaming; except. . .
Prince Except what, my love?
Helga It feels more like waking up.
Prince The same thing, Helga. Come closer.
(*fade up – sharpening of axe*)
Mother Thorstein! Whatever are you up to?
Father Just sharpening my axe.
Mother What for?
Father I'm going out wood-cutting.
Mother Going out what?
Father I'm bored; I want something to do – We've been here weeks if not months and I'm getting fat and flabby.
Mother But what will the servants think? Give me that axe.
Father No you don't! The days are too long and too level. I've got to pass the time somehow.

Helga Pass the time, kill the time, pass the time, kill the time – If Time were a baby chicken I'd wring his baby neck! The days are too long when one's all by oneself. Not a breath of the open air, not a single window to look through. Only my own reflection over and over in the gold-framed mirrors. The nights now – the nights are different. If only I could see what he looks like – but it always has to be dark and he's always gone before dawn. My own . . . my own invisible! But these days between are a desert.
Bear Gf, Helga! What's wrong?
Helga Oh you made me jump. Nothing's wrong.
Bear Gf! I can read your eyes.
Helga It's only I want to see my family.
Bear Your family?
Helga What's strange about that?
Bear Gf! Nothing strange. Just dangerous.

Helga Dangerous!

Bear Gf! Mistaken.

Helga Couldn't you take me to see them?

Bear Gf! I could. But promise me one thing.

Helga Anything. Anything to see them.

Bear Promise you won't talk alone with your mother. If you do, it's bad luck for both of us. Promise?

Helga Talk alone with my mother? Of course not. The one I want to talk to's Halvor.

Bear Promise?

Helga Oh you are a bear! Yes, I promise not to talk alone with my mother.

Bear Right. Get on my back.

(*fade up reverberating bell*)

Mother Visitors! Where's my tiara? Thorstein, light your golden pipe, man. Halvor, sit up and do your sums — on your slate with the golden frame round it.

Halvor The sums aren't golden, mother.

Father Now who the devil can be calling? No one calls on us here.

Mother That's your fault, Thorstein. You don't live up to this castle.

Father If you mean that I've kept a sense of proportion –

Halvor Oh look! Look! Helga!

Father Helga!

Mother Well, this is a surprise. Be careful now how you kiss me.

Helga Oh mother, father, Halvor, how wonderful to see you again!

Mother Let's have a look at you, Helga. . . Aye, you're thinner. And shadows under your eyes. What kind of a place are you living in? A lair or a den or a cave or a bear-pit –

Helga A wonderful, wonderful castle. It's inside a hill and –

Father Inside a hill!

Helga With hundreds and hundreds of rooms in it.

Mother Hundreds? Of big rooms?

Helga Oh yes, bigger than this.

Mother This is one of our wee ones. Wait till I take you round the others.

Helga Yes, I'd love to see them later.

Mother Come on. No time like the present.

Helga Coming, father?

Father No, no, I'll wait here. I find these marble floors somewhat tiring on the feet. Besides, I've got to make this golden pipe draw.

Halvor I'll come, Helga.

53

Mother No you don't! You concentrate on your arithmetic. Now where will I take you first? Into my boudoir, I think.

Halvor She wants to show you her parrot.

Helga You keep a parrot in your boudoir?

Mother Aye certainly; it's company.

Father Very distinguished company. It wears a diamond collar.

Helga Mother, I'm tired from my journey. Couldn't I see it later?

Mother If you wait too long, it might die. They say it's a hundred years old.

Halvor And it's never laid an egg.

Mother That's because it's an it. Come on now, Helga. That's the girl.

Parrot (*whistles*) Gold and silver – pearls and diamonds – silk and satin – gold and silver.

Mother You see. It's almost human.

Parrot Gold and silver – pearls and diamonds – silk and sat-, silk and sat-, silk and sat-, silk and sick-up! (*vomiting noise, squawk, silence*)

Mother What did I tell you! It's died.

Helga Oh mother, how sad!

Mother Ach, it'd only have interrupted us. Now we can discuss the burning question.

Helga What burning question?

Mother This bear of yours. Has he, er . . . has he, er. . .?

Helga No mother. I only see him in the daytime – and not very often then.

Mother Then you're all alone at night?

Helga Oh yes, mother; it's dark, you see.

Mother What's that got to do with it?

Helga Well, er, it's only a dream of course.

Mother What is?

Helga He is.

Mother Who is?

(*pause*)

Helga, you're keeping something from me. He? Who's he? And what is he? What is his station in life?

Helga I can't answer so many questions at a time.

Mother Then one at a time. What does he look like?

Helga Oh, I don't know what he looks like. All I know is he's wonderful.

Mother All you know is –! He might be a troll.

Helga He's not a troll!

Mother Seeing is believing. Look, I'll give you a candle. Tonight when he's asleep, light it – but be sure not to drop the tallow on him. If

54

he's a troll you'll see and if he's a prince you'll see – not that it's likely he'd be a prince with those shadows under your eyes –

Helga A prince? But he *is* a prince! The most beautiful prince in the world! So beautiful I must kiss him – but gently so I don't wake him –
   (*kiss and symbolic effect*)

Prince Oh! I'm burnt.

Helga Oh dear!

Prince What have you done, Helga? Didn't I warn you not to talk with your mother?

Helga *You* didn't warn me. It was the bear.

Prince I am the bear, Helga. Bear by day and man by night. An enchantment laid upon me by my stepmother; she is a troll, a very powerful one. If you'd only held out for the rest of this year the spell would have been broken and I should have been myself again. But now what is broken is between us two. And I must go back to my stepmother and marry a different princess.

Helga A different – What is she like?

Prince She has green hair, webbed fingers, bad breath, a squint, a stutter, tusks in her mouth, whiskers in her ears, and a nose that is three yards long. She is a troll too, you see.

Helga I see. (*sobs*) Where does your stepmother live?

Prince In a castle like no other castle in a place that is past finding. East of the sun and west of the moon and there I must go this minute.

Helga I will come with you.

Prince Impossible.

Helga Then tell me the way and I'll follow you.

Prince There is no way. Ask anyone that and they'll tell you so.

Helga Ask anyone? I'll ask everyone!

Prince Goodbye.

Helga But kiss me!

Prince I can't. It is forbidden. This is the end. For you. For me. For everyone.
   (*thunder clap*)

Mother Thorstein! Wake up!

Father What is it?

Mother I think we've been struck by lightning.

Father Eh! What's happened to this bed? It's so small you're pushing me out of it. And where are the mattress and the sheets and the pillows –

Halvor (*off*) Mother! Father! Where are you? The rain's coming through the roof on me.

Mother The rain? Through the roof? Thorstein, light the lamp on the night table.

Father Just a moment. . . Can't find it. . . Sorry, no lamp, no night table.

Mother In the name of St Nicholas of Lost Property –

Halvor Mother, I'm dying of cold. All the blankets have gone from my bed.

Mother Come over here then.

Halvor I can't see where you are. Ow!

Father What have you done?

Halvor Put my foot through the floor.

> (*thunder clap*)

Mother Did you see that?

Father The lightning? Of course I did.

Mother No, you fool. Did you see this room in the flash of it? We're back where we started, Thorstein. In rags in the cottage in the valley in the mist in misery. (*sobs*) Aye, the story's over for us.

Father What story?. . . Oh, never mind.

Singer East of the sun and west of the moon –
None can reach it late or soon;
How to find it is known to none,
West of the moon and east of the sun.

West of the moon and east of the sun,
Take your compass or take your gun,
Find it you may not night or noon,
East of the sun and west of the moon.

> (*cross-fade into cock-crow*)

Helga (*waking up*) Where am I?. . . What a lovely morning! But what am I doing out here, my hair's just drenched with the dew? Have I been walking in my sleep? And carrying my pillow with me? Pillow? But it's my bundle! The same old bundle of rags I brought with me when the bear – the bear? The prince! Last night! The candle! The burning tallow! (*pause*) A lovely morning? I wish I was dead.

First Crone And why do you wish that?

Helga Oh!

First Crone Don't be frightened. I know I frighten people, I suppose it's because I'm so old. Ninety last Hallowe'en. That's when I won this golden apple; we were ducking for it in a tub and I caught it between my nose and chin. But I mustn't talk about myself. Why do you wish you were dead?

Helga I've lost my lover.

First Crone Then go and find him.

Helga I can't. He lives with his stepmother. In a castle that's east of –

First Crone East of the sun and west of the moon. Ha! ha! ha! ha! ha! At long first and at first last though spirit be willing flesh is weak and what you seek is never to find and what you find is never to hold and what you hold is never to spend – No, child, you'll never get there!

Helga Never?

First Crone Never all but a day. You can always try the all but.

Helga But how do I start?

First Crone On my horse here. I'll lend him to you, I'm long past riding anyway. He'll take you to another old lady, she's older than I am, she may know the way.

Helga Oh thank you, thank you –

First Crone And by the way, you may take this golden apple. It might come in handy some day.

> (*hoof effects combined with rhythmical whispering voice – 'East of the sun', etc. and behind*)

Helga Mile upon mile upon mile – and this is only the beginning.

> (*hoofs to stop*)

Good morning, grandmother.

Second Crone Morning.

Helga May I ask you if you know the way –

Second Crone Don't distract me when I'm combing my hair. It won't take long; as you see, there's not much of it. Strand of six hairs – strand of three hairs – strand of two – and finis!

Helga What a lovely gold comb!

Second Crone Yes, wasted on me really.

Helga Oh no, I always think old ladies –

Second Crone Don't you dare call me an old lady. Fine words bring back nothing. Not one lost hair to the scalp, nor one lost tooth to the gums, nor one drop of blood to the veins. Old lady indeed! I'm a hag, a horror, a crone. If my grandson could see me now, the poor boy would turn in his grave. You wanted to ask me something?

Helga Only the way to –

Second Crone Your prince's stepmother's castle east of the sun and –

Helga How did you guess?

Second Crone Because you're the girl that ought to have had him but – ha! ha! ha! – curiosity killed the cat.

Helga If you know so much, then you must know the way.

Second Crone Don't be impertinent. There are certain things I prefer not to know. But if you ride on a bit – and then a bit more for bad measure – you'll find someone less particular. She was born in a less particular age; I'm only a hundred, you see. You ask *her* – if she can hear you still. Oh, and take this golden comb with you. A golden comb can sort out many tangles.

    (*hoofs, with voice, and behind*)

Helga Oh, what a long, long way – and it's *still* only the beginning!

    (*hoofs to stop*)

    But there's no one here!

Third Crone No one?

Helga I'm sorry, I thought –

Third Crone You thought no doubt I was an inanimate object. Yes, it's fifty years since I looked like a human being. Can you spin?

Helga Spin?

Third Crone My hands are too feeble for it now and it's difficult with no eyes. I was spinning thread for my shroud but it needs just one more day's work. Spin for me today and I'll reward you.

Helga But where's your spinning-wheel?

Third Crone Under my skirt. Here!

Helga But it's of gold!

Third Crone That's why it's under my skirt. When I was a girl gold spinning-wheels were all the rage. In court circles, that is. What are you waiting for? There's the wheel, here's the wool; if you can spin, spin!

    (*spinning effect and fade out, then fade up again and to close*)

    Thank you; you don't spin badly. Well, I shan't need this spinning-wheel again; you can take it with you for your wages.

Helga Oh, thank you! But can you also –

Third Crone No, I can't. I can only advise you to ride on – and on – be it with your heart in your mouth, be it with your tongue in your cheek – till you come to the East Wind. Maybe he knows those parts and will blow you there.

Helga Thank you very much. Before I leave, may I ask you something?

Third Crone Is it personal?

Helga Well, yes it is, I'm afraid. You remind me so much of the last two people I met.

Third Crone The last two people? Ha! ha! ha! I'm a hundred and fifty, my child. But fifty years ago I was a hundred. And sixty years ago I was ninety.

Helga If you mean what I think you mean . . . but then how would I fit in?

Third Crone Why shouldn't you?

Helga But I'm still young.

Third Crone Your youth is your nature. That's all part of the story.

Helga What story?

Third Crone You'll know when you've lived it. As I have. Now get on that horse. Good luck to you.

(*hoof effects, with voice, and behind*)

Helga Oh, I'm so stiff. Why must that East Wind live so far away?

(*hoofs to stop*)

East Wind Good morning, Princess-ji. I am knowing to what I owe the honour of this visit. Kindly sit here under the flame-tree.

Helga Thank you.

East Wind Yes, it is a matter of transportation – quite a commitment, jolly tough puff. And always it is not on the maps.

Helga But you can blow me there, can you?

East Wind Princess-ji, you must not jump conclusions. I am not what I was, I fear; if only I had served my guru as I have served my nautch girl – Excuse, Princess-ji, I forget myself. Now I will give you your garland.

Helga But I don't want garlands, all I want is –

East Wind More haste less speed, is it not? There! Roses and marigolds.

Helga But they tickle.

East Wind No, keep it on please. And now to business. This business I think I will delegate.

Helga To whom?

East Wind To my colleague the West Wind. Very strapping chap, good acceleration and stamina. Always highly thought of by meteorology department.

Helga Where can I find him?

East Wind Very long journey, I fear.

Helga How many days' ride?

59

East Wind Ride? On horseback you are meaning?

    Helga If you'll just give him some oats, he –

East Wind Oats! No, for this trip oat-power is out of the question. If you do not mind the piggyback, we will make this relay race.

    Helga It's very kind of you.

East Wind Not at all, Princess-ji; it is all in the day's blow. I had been meaning to whip up the Bay of Bengal but that can wait till tomorrow. To-morrow, as the poet says – Tomorrow is tomorrow is tomorrow. You will have to hold on by my hair though.

    Helga Can we start now?

East Wind One moment. Is that a golden comb you have? Be so kind please as to run it once through my wings.

    Helga Like this?

East Wind Like that. The streamlined effect is a functional. Now please like-wise the other wing.

    Helga Sorry, I didn't mean to tug.

East Wind It is the ghee makes clots of the feathers. That will do nicely. Now kindly mount my shoulder-blades. Good. Hold tight. We are off!

    (East Wind flight and to stop)

West Wind Will you look who's here! To come blustering in like that, dis-turbing my afternoon nap and the beautiful dream I was having. I was dreaming about nine bean rows –

East Wind My broth of a colleague, attend please. This lady that I disembark from my shoulders always is wishing to obtain information –

West Wind About that castle? Sorry, Miss; I've never blown that far. And I wouldn't want to from what I've heard of the place. There's castles and castles but that one beats all.

    Helga Beats all for what?

West Wind For nastiness. Shadows and monsters and dungeons and tortures. And things so bad you wouldn't find them in the dictionary. Why any nice girl in her senses should –

    Helga My prince is there.

West Wind Ah, that's different. Look now – for what it's worth – suppose I take you to the South Wind? I hate to admit it but he's stronger than me. Or not stronger exactly, just in better training.

East Wind Jolly good idea!

    Helga It is!

East Wind But be careful of this fellow; he bucks.

West Wind Buck! I do no such thing. Come on, Miss; jump up. Give her a hand, ye ould avatar. Right. We're under starter's order.

60

East Wind Wait please till I make the mudra. Princess-ji and old boy, stand
by. One; two; three and –
    (*West Wind's flight, and to stop*)

South Wind Mamma Mia! Signorina, you honour me. I beg you be seated.
Now what can I do for you? You like the coffee? You like the
cake? You like the wine?

West Wind She likes the way to the castle that's east of –

South Wind I do not like that way.

Helga Why, have you ever been there?

South Wind No, but I still do not like it. E brutto, quello castellaccio. The owls,
the bones, the nightmares!

Helga Who told you about it?

South Wind My collega, Signor Borea, the North Wind. I think he goes there
one time.

West Wind Is that a fact? Well, it's an ill wind that – You take this young lady
along to him.

South Wind With pleasure of course but this North Wind – Signorina, he has
the bad manner; we do not, how one says it, mix.

West Wind To hell with how one says it mix! She's in love, can't you see, she's
in love.

South Wind Naturalmente. I see it well and you see it but Borea –

West Wind You must take a chance on it.

Helga Oh please, please! Take a chance on it.

South Wind I do it. Your hair is so gold, your voice is so gentle, your eyes are
so blue, your heart is so sad, I do it! We take off now from this
balcony. Be brave, signorina. Avanti!
    (*South Wind's flight and to stop*)
Ecco! We are arrived. The palazzo of Signor Borea.

Helga What funny-looking glass the windows are made of!

South Wind Not glass, signorina. Ice.

Helga Look, someone's opening the door.
    (*bursts of wind to synchronise with North Wind and behind*)

North Wind (*calling*) Blast you both! What do you want?

South Wind (*calling*) Borea, sono io.

North Wind (*calling*) What?

South Wind (*calling*) It is me.

North Wind (*calling*) I can see it is. Who's that wench?

South Wind (*calling*) The signorina who loses her lover to the castle east of –

North Wind (*calling*) Oh, that one! All right. Come up here.
    (*wind increases*)

61

  Helga I can hardly stand up.

South Wind Endure – till we are indoors. Indoors he stops blowing.

North Wind Hm! You look cold. Come in.

    (*door closes; wind out*)

    Sit down. Sorry I've no chairs. Now what's the trouble?

South Wind The trouble? I tell you.

North Wind No you don't. Where's that blasted groom? It's getting dark. Groom!

  Groom Here, sir.

North Wind Light the icicles. Continue.

South Wind The trouble –

North Wind Not you. Her.

  Helga Please, sir, I hear you once went to the castle that –

North Wind Once is enough. I was younger then – I'm the oldest of the winds, you know – but once I did blow an aspen leaf there, but I was so tired I was puffed out for weeks. No, it's not worth it; I've better things to do. Tomorrow I'm proposing to blow down a pine forest.

South Wind But that you do as you go. Between here and the castle must be hundreds of forests –

North Wind I'm not going back to that castle. Once is enough, I tell you.

  Helga Once is enough when you're blowing an aspen leaf. But when it means saving the man that one loves –

North Wind *I* don't love him. Why should I?

  Helga Because he comes from the north – like you do.

North Wind From the north, eh? Thought he was a wog.

South Wind Borea!

North Wind Whereabouts in the north? Tundra or mountain?

  Helga Mountain.

North Wind Good. Does he drink ale?

  Helga I think so.

South Wind Si, si! He drinks much ale.

North Wind And mead?

  Helga Yes, gallons of mead.

North Wind And breaks the ice for his morning dip in the fjord?

  Helga Oh, yes – and his evening dip too. And sometimes he dips at midnight.

North Wind Excellent. What's his favourite dish?

  Helga Oh, er, whale-meat.

North Wind Raw?

Helga Of course. And he catches his whale single-handed.

North Wind Does he, by Thor!

South Wind And he throws the bones at the servants.

North Wind Ah, the good old days! I remember once I was calling on a family in England – Danish family of course. . . Where was I? I was making up my mind.

Helga Oh, were you!

North Wind Yes, but what about? Ah, to be sure, your young man. Throws the bones at the servants, eh? Yes, I've a good mind to help you.

Helga Oh, how wonderful! How can I ever –

North Wind You'll have to sleep here tonight though. Take us a whole day to get there. Now where's that blasted groom?

Groom Here, sir.

North Wind Out with your currycomb, man. Quick as you can or I'll blast you all over the heath. I want you to rub me down. Big job on tomorrow.

> (*pause*)
> (*North Wind's flight – spaced out with dialogue*)

Don't fall off. Air pockets ahead.

Ha! ha! See that town? Not a roof left on a house in it!

Hm. Nice stretch of forest. *Was* nice. Take 'em years to replace it.

Hold on now. Going to cross the ocean. Calling all ships; this is Force Thirteen. Ha! There goes the first ship.

Two – three – four – (*fade him*)

Good bag that! Seven hundred and ninety-two. So much for that ocean. Next one's even wider.

Helga (*gasping*) Please don't sink any more ships.

North Wind Next ocean has no ships. No name either. Mankind never discovered it.

> (*cross-fade effects into singer*)

Singer East of the sun and west of the moon
Cross the sea like a black typhoon,
Fly through the sky till your race be run
West of the moon and east of the sun.

West of the moon and east of the sun
Fly till you die or your task be done.
Summer or winter, night or noon,
East of the sun and west of the moon.

(cross-fade singer into effects)

Helga   Am I imagining it – or are you going slower?

North Wind   Shade slower, yes. But don't be afraid. Hold on. We should just make land before nightfall. *(to self)* Slower! I'll soon be at a stand-still. Losing height too. Serious.

    (splash)

Helga   Oh what was that?

North Wind   Sorry, did I splash you? Careless of me.

    (to self) Losing height? My feet are hitting the wave-tops!

    (series of splashes)

Helga   Look! Land! Land!

North Wind   Can't see a thing. Where?

Helga   Straight ahead of us.

North Wind   Good.

    (to self) Keep going now, keep going. Both wings at once. Breast-stroke.

Helga   Oh!

North Wind   Hold on, Helga. We'll do the last lap by water.

    (churning of water)

Helga   Oh, don't let's drown at the last –

North Wind   Drown? I'm in my depth! Hold on, Helga, we'll walk it. Water to my neck . . . my midriff . . . my hips . . . knees . . . ankles . . . There, what did I tell you!

Helga   East of the sun and west of the moon! We've got there!

    (thud of large falling body)

    Oh, he's fainted.

North Wind   Fainted? Certainly not. Just slipped on the seaweed and jelly-fish.

Helga   Can I help you up?

North Wind   No. Bedtime. I'll stay where I am on the seaweed. Dark night, isn't it?

Helga   Yes. And there's something still darker up there.

    (owl hoots)

North Wind   What's that? Owl in a tree?

Helga   Owl on a castle rampart. The castle where *he* is . . . where *those* are. The castle that *I* must get into tomorrow.

    (more owls and fade)

Stepmother   Longnose my dear! Why are you standing at that window? What are you staring at?

Longnose   A beggar girl. In the ditch there among the rubbish.

Stepmother   A beggar girl! Don't hurt your eyes, Longnose.

Longnose She's got a big golden apple.

Stepmother A what?

Longnose She's throwing it up and catching it.

Stepmother Why, you're right.

Longnose I'm going to have that apple. Hey, beggar girl!

Helga (*off*) Yes?

Longnose What do you want for your golden apple?

Helga It's not for sale – not for gold or silver.

Longnose Then what about pearls and rubies? I have them the size of hen's eggs.

Helga It's not for sale – in pearls or rubies.

Longnose Diamonds and emeralds?

Helga Not diamonds nor emeralds.

Longnose Name your own price then.

Stepmother Longnose!

Longnose I'll give you anything you want.

Helga Is there a prince that lives in this castle?

Stepmother Careful, Longnose –

Longnose There is.

Helga Allow me to spend tonight in his room.

Longnose It's a bargain.

Helga The apple is yours.

Stepmother Not very wise, my dear –

Helga Catch?

(*golden apple falling and rolling on floor*)

Stepmother Butterfingers! As I was saying –

Longnose Oh, look at it, stepmother mine to be.

Stepmother Yes, but is it worth it? That beggar girl all night in his room –

Longnose Have you forgotten your sleeping-draught? We'll give it him before he goes to bed and –

Stepmother Longnose, my child, you'll make an excellent wife.

Longnose Ha! ha! ha! Nothing will wake him tonight.

(*fiddle*)

Helga But my love, my own white bear! Wake up, it's Helga! Helga! . . . No use. Oh, St Harald the Wakener! Not even you could wake him tonight. And not even burning tallow! (*sobs*) More beautiful even than ever – but frozen like a body in a glacier. If only he'd wake, I'd sooner have him a bear again. To think I've come all this long, long way for this! The first old hag, the second old hag, the third. East Wind, West Wind, South Wind, North Wind. And

65

C

into this evil castle where things mutter in the chimney and the walls keep moving in and out and the ceilings keep rising and sinking and the figures on the tapestries never keep still and everything's clammy to the touch. Wake up, my heart – three hours I've been begging you . . . four hours . . . five hours . . . six hours . . . seven –

Longnose Come on, come on, time's up! Out you go, you slut. Back to the castle ditch with you.

(*fade up North Wind yawning*)

North Wind Hm, excellent sleep. Still not fit enough to fly though. (*sneezes*) Seem to have caught a cold. Ha! ha! Me! A cold! (*sneezes*) 'm, what's this knot in my handkerchief? Ah to be sure, Helga; I was keeping her golden comb for her. Had to deliver it somewhere. . . Ah yes, the castle ditch. Sun's well up, I must hurry.

Longnose Hey you snub-nosed slut! What's that you're combing your hair with?

Helga It's not for sale in –

Longnose Name your price and hand over.

(*fade up owls, then fade out, pause, and fade up cock*)

North Wind Helga, here's the spinning-wheel. Third time lucky, my girl.

Helga I don't believe it. He's enchanted.

North Wind Enchanted? Probably doped.

Helga Anyway, he won't wake. But I'll try; it's my last chance. He's to be married tomorrow.

Prisoner You must believe me, prince. This is your last chance.

Prince But there's only one girl it could be – and for her I'd wake at the shadow of a whisper.

Prisoner Why should I lie when it puts me in danger? I'm a captive in this castle – as you are, and I'm a Christian – as you are. I tell you I sleep in the next room to yours and two nights running she's kept me awake. All the night through imploring and weeping –

Prince I have it! The drink!

Prisoner What drink?

Prince The drink that these two nights past Longnose has brought me at bedtime. Well, I can cheat her tonight.

Longnose My husband to be tomorrow, here is your spiced wine.

Prince Thank you. Spiced is the word for it. In raising it now to my lips – Good Hell! What's that behind you?

Longnose What?

(*slight splash*)

66

There was nothing.

Prince Must have been an optical illusion. I've noticed several in this castle.

Longnose You drank that very quickly.

Prince Couldn't help it. And now, Longnose, my bride of tomorrow, forgive me if I go to bed. I can hardly keep my eyes open.

Longnose Good. You must sleep well for tomorrow. And what a surprise you will have when you see the great hall laid out for our wedding. Your stepmother kept it a secret. She's had all the prisoners at work for a week, scrubbing and polishing and hanging decorations.

Prince So you see, my love, the great hall is our battlefield. And the plan of campaign is this. You remember that tallow candle –

Helga Oh, don't! Don't remind me!

Prince But this is what will save us. I still have the shirt I was wearing that night and it still has three spots of tallow on it. Before the wedding I'll ask Longnose to wash it. She'll accept of course, but she'll fail. A Christian dropped the tallow, so only a Christian can wash it away. And certainly none of these trolls. When they've all failed, I'll call upon you, Helga.

Helga Yes, of course, I'll wash it for you. Now hug me, my own white bear – close as an eyelid on an eye. Forget all those trolls till tomorrow.

(*jibbering of trolls and behind*)

Stepmother Well, my stepson. How do you like my decorations?

Prince That centre piece of skulls is nice.

Stepmother I didn't have quite enough old bones so I slaughtered a couple more prisoners. And what about the pythons hanging from the chandeliers – they need watching, of course, one's just swallowed our dwarf. And the toads swimming in the finger bowls? And the toadstools I've grown on the wedding cake? And those vultures I've specially trained to – Whatever is that in your hand?

Prince It's a shirt – the finest linen. I wanted to wear it today but it has these three spots of tallow –

Stepmother How did they get on it?

Prince Oh, I can't remember.

Stepmother Well they're very small spots. Of course you'll wear it today. I'll call the washerwoman.

Prince No. I've suddenly had an idea. Let's see what Longnose is fit for. I've always thought that a wife should –

67

Stepmother Longnose can wash beautifully. Longnose, my dear, come here!

Longnose Yes?

Stepmother This shirt. Your prince wishes to wear it but –

Prince I thought you might wash it for me, Longnose.

Longnose If I couldn't, I'd be no wife for you. Bring me the tub. I'll have that shirt clean in a minute.

 (*fade up scrubbing and splashing and behind*)

Prince A minute, did you say?

Stepmother Longnose, what's wrong with you!

Longnose I've nearly finished it.

Prince Have you?

Longnose Tallow? Very queer tallow!

Prince I think those spots are getting larger.

Stepmother I believe they are. And blacker. No, my poor girl, you're a charlatan – no bride for a stepson of mine. Give me that shirt. I insist. Now *I'll* show you how to wash shirts!

 (*up effects and behind*)

Prince They're still getting larger.

Stepmother They're not!

Prince They're blacker.

Stepmother They're not!

Longnose They are!

Stepmother Hold your tongue, Longnose.

 (*slap and shriek*)

Prince I think you're just wasting time; those three spots have all run together now. Look at this shirt, you'd think it had been up the chimney. Can't anyone here wash? Come on! . . . What, no takers? Why, I thought trolls could do everything. What about you, ma'am?

Female Troll Opschki barrabom natch kickery no-no.

Prince And you, sir?

Male Troll Allaby hamgut allaby phonikon allaby kotskop allaby no-no!

Troll Crowd No-no, no-no, no-no, no-no. NO-NO!

Prince But I *will* have this shirt washed. The first girl that does it can marry me. Even if she is a beggar girl.

Helga (*approaching*) Like me?

Prince Who're you?

Helga A beggar girl.

Prince Right. Will you try?

Helga I'll try.

68

Prince Watch, Longnose. Watch, Stepmother.
    (*washing effects and behind*)
Helga I dip it in like this, I rub it like this, I wring it like this, I rinse it
    again and – there!
Crowd (*troll reactions*)
Stepmother Witchcraft!
Prince *You* talk of witchcraft!
Stepmother I do. Now I'll show you mine. If you think you're going to marry
    that human –
Trolls No-no, no-no, no-no, no-no, NO-NO!
Stepmother In the name of the ancient frost giants, I the queen of this castle –
    (*burst of wind*)
North Wind Hold it there!
Stepmother Who are you?
North Wind I am the North Wind and I blew down your frost giants long ago.
    Well, I've just had three nights and two days rest and I feel like
    blowing down this castle.
Stepmother I defy you.
North Wind You do? Pf!
    (*popping effect*)
Crowd (*troll gasps of astonishment*)
Helga Why, she's exploded... Do it to Longnose.
North Wind With pleasure. Pf!
    (*pop*)
Helga That will teach her.
Crowd (*panic-stricken jabbering of trolls*)
North Wind Look at them all. Never saw such a bunch. Blue ones, green ones,
    spiky ones, scaly ones – Pf! Pf! Pf! Pf! Pf! Pf! etc.
    (*punctuating this with pops, accelerating, then petering out*)
    There. Good riddance. Place still stinks though. I tell you what:
    you two release the prisoners and take any jewels you fancy and
    get out fast before I blow properly. Wait for me outside – not too
    near though.
    (*pause, fade up effect of collapsing castle*)
Prince That's it. Now we wait for him. Did he mean he'd carry us home?
Helga Of course he did, love. But where *is* home?
Prince Anywhere you and I are.
Helga But that would mean even here! Oh wherever's that sweet smell
    coming from?
Prince Look at the ground.

69

Helga Flowers! But just now this was cinders.

Prince Since then he's blown down the castle.

Helga Snowdrops, violets, roses – all the seasons mixed up!

Prince Look what's happening in the sky! The sun's shining – but so are the stars.

North Wind (*approaching*) Well, what are you two staring at? Little lovers' head in air! Come on, get on my back.

Helga No, thank you, dear Wind.

Prince We're not coming.

North Wind Not coming!

Helga We're staying here among the flowers.

North Wind Flowers?

Helga Can't you see them?

North Wind No.

Prince Nor the stars?

North Wind Of course not. At midday?

Helga We can see them.

North Wind Extraordinary! Still *I* was in love once. Look after yourselves. Goodbye.

Both Goodbye.

Helga And thank you again.

North Wind (*off*) Thank *you*. It was an experience.

Helga So here we are.

Prince Home.

Helga Home.

Singer East of the sun and west of the moon
What was midnight now is noon,
Hate is ended, love begun,
West of the moon and east of the sun.

West of the moon and east of the sun
Green trees dance and bright streams run,
All our years combine in June
East of the sun and west of the moon

West of the moon and east of the sun
Tale is over, thread is spun;
Seek it yourself – it's Why and How –
East of never, west of now.
(*piano*) Seek it yourself – it's why and how –
East of never, west of now.

They Met on Good Friday

A Sceptical Historical Romance

First broadcast in the BBC Third Programme on 8 December 1959 in Louis MacNeice's production, with music by Tristram Cary and the following cast:

OLD WOMAN	*Bee Duffell*
THORSTEIN	*James McKechnie*
EARL SIGURD	*Patrick Wymark*
SIGTRYG	*Denys Hawthorne*
BISHOP	*Brian O'Higgins*
GORMLAI	*Kathleen Michael*
KING BRIAN	*Patrick Magee*
HARPER	*Robert Mooney*
POET	*Robert Irwin*
HALGERDA	*Mary Wimbush*
SLAVE GIRL	*Sheila Brennan*
ETAIN	*Patricia Leventon*
BRODIR	*Kenneth J. Warren*
MURAGH	*P. G. Stephens*
MAEL SEACHLAINN	*Eamonn Keane*
CAPTAIN OF THE GUARD	*Rio Fanning*
TURLOUGH	*Donal Donnelly*

with members of the BBC Drama Repertory Company

Announcer In the ninth and tenth centuries AD the vikings exploded on
Europe – nobody quite knows why. From Scandinavia they set
out in their long ships to burn and loot, to ravish and murder, and
sometimes even to colonise. They settled in the Scottish islands, in
Iceland, and northern England; in AD 1013 they actually conquered
England. In the following year, in Ireland – a country they had
long been plundering and where they had founded several still
famous cities – they fought their greatest battle and met their
greatest defeat on 23 April, Good Friday, AD 1014. There were
Norsemen fighting on the Irish side and Irishmen fighting on the
Norse side and in several of the protagonists the blood of the two
races was mingled. Still, the two armies stood for two different
ways of life and thought no doubt they were deciding something
when: They Met on Good Friday.

(harp overture, leading into sea music and behind)

Old Woman The horses of the sea . . . the horses of the sea . . . the black and
whinnying horses of the sea. . . Their manes are tangled and their
teeth are long and their wind is long and their ears are back. And
they never quit, they never quit.

Child They never quit?

Old Woman Changing the coasts of Ireland. You see these pebbles, child?
When I was your age, they were big stones. And you see this stone
the size of a handmill? When I was your age it was a boulder. But
the waves have whittled them down with their hoofs. No one can
fight the sea.

Child Not even Cuchullain?

Old Woman Aye, *he* fought the sea. But he lost.

Child Not even King Brian?

Old Woman Listen. King Brian is my age. People speak well of him now but I
know the things he has done. And I know the things he has not
done. Put him out there and the horses would trample him under.
And so would the dragons that follow the horses.

Child Dragons?

Old Woman The dragon ships, child. The horses' jaws are yellow with foam
but the dragons' jaws are red with blood. When I was your age
there was an old woman who had been carried away by one of
those slavering dragons, sixty years back when her cheeks still had

73
C*

colour. Carried away to some land of ice. But when her cheeks were losing their colour they sold her back to a Dublin merchant. Sold her back for a bundle of hides. And this will all happen again.

Child I don't understand.

Old Woman Mark my words, a little bird told me. A wren in an ash tree, a crow on a grave – or ask those gulls, they know it surely. Not a few weeks from now the dragons will ride up this beach. For the spearmen, death, for the virgins, rape, for the monasteries, fire, for King Brian, defeat.

Child But –

Old Woman You don't believe it. Nor do many. Mark my words: at this very moment they are pitching their timbers and painting their prows. To be strong for the brine, to be spruce for the kill.

(lose music)

Thorstein Grey? Grey, you dauber! Why can't you use your red and your gold? Call yourself a ship's painter! Call that a dragon – it looks more like a lemming. Give me the brush; I'll teach you your trade.

Painter Lemmings go west, too.

Thorstein Now . . . gold for the scales.

Painter Lemmings go west and they drown. And no man, Thorstein, knows what drives them. Small foolish creatures; they swim out west till they drown. You're dipping too deep; you are blurring the outline.

Thorstein Hold your tongue or I'll knock your teeth out. Blurring the – Wait till we grapple them! The bay of Dublin will be blurred with blood and the outlines of Ireland drawn anew. The red paint? Where's the red?

Painter In front of you.

Thorstein Hold your tongue! Now for his eyes – make them bloodshot. As they were last year when we sailed for England. Landed at Gainsborough, soaked up Oxford and Winchester, Bath and London fell on their knees to us, the English King escaped to Normandy.

Painter I have never been to England.

Thorstein You have never been anywhere, oaf. Look at the grey sea yonder – What is it for? To take men – who call themselves men – to harry the coasts of the world. As it took our forebears to Lisbon and Cadiz. As thirty years back it took Eric the Red to Greenland. As thirty days on it will take this dragon to Orkney.

Painter Orkney? I thought you were going to Ireland.

74

Thorstein Orkney, fool, lies on the way to Ireland. It is there that things shall be decided. Things, fool. Matters of history.

Music (*Viking horn, used heraldically*)

Herald Silence in the Earl's Hall! The meeting will now be resumed. The word lies with Sigurd, Earl of Orkney.

Sigurd Sigtryg of the Silken Beard, I speak to you man to man. Your mother is an Irish queen; I also had an Irish mother. Blood these days keeps mingling – if not on the field, in the bed. You call me to Ireland to lead the host of the vikings. I know your reasons; you are in fear of King Brian who was lately your mother's husband – her third husband, am I right?

Sigtryg Earl Sigurd of Orkney, all her husbands were kings. Her first was my father, Olaf, King of Dublin. Her second Mael Seachlainn, once High King of Ireland –

Sigurd Who still lives?

Sigtryg Who still lives. Her third Brian, now High King of Ireland.

Sigurd Who still lives. So far so good – or so bad. What about her fourth?

Sigtryg Her fourth?

Sigurd He should be a king, too. If I do what you ask me to do, if I come to Ireland and defeat King Brian, I demand in return the hand of your mother Gormlai – and with it the throne of Dublin. Well?

(*pause*)

Sigtryg The throne of Dublin is supposed to be mine.

Sigurd 'Supposed' to be? Yes. In the old days the Norsemen in Dublin were free. You, Sigtryg of the Silken Beard, it is you who paid tribute to Brian. And only last Christmas, when he laid siege to Dublin, it was no thanks to you he withdrew. Had it not been that the winter was cold and the Irish ran short of food, our chief Norse market in the west would be lost; Dublin, the city which our fathers founded, Dublin, that jewel of the viking world, would no longer be Norse – but Irish! And among its charred ruins there would squat a race of beggars, their hair falling into their eyes, their fingers in bowls of porridge, their tongues never still, back-biting each other and all men. What do you say, Thorstein?

Thorstein I say that Sigtryg has forfeited his kingdom –

Sigtryg Thorstein!

Sigurd Let him speak.

Thorstein He is not strong enough to hold our city of Dublin. His greatest

75

asset is his mother, Gormlai, but to you she would be a far stronger asset. Besides, she is still beautiful.

Sigurd Yes, I have heard of the lady. But this time – no divorce.

Sigtryg Does that mean, Earl Sigurd. . .

Sigurd Yes?

Sigtryg Does that mean you are accepting my offer?

Sigurd Repeat your offer. We must have things clear.

Sigtryg I, Sigtryg, the King of Dublin –

Sigurd At present King of Dublin.

Sigtryg I, Sigtryg, at present King of Dublin, hereby invite Earl Sigurd of Orkney to rally the fighters of the viking world – from Norway, from Denmark, from Ireland, the Hebrides, Orkney and Man, and from all parts whatever – and to lead the same against Ireland there to do battle with King Brian who has done such harm to our people. In return for which. . .

Sigurd Yes?

Sigtryg When he has defeated Brian, I promise him the throne of Dublin – and the hand of my mother Gormlai.

(*pause*)

You accept my offer?

Sigurd You accept my conditions?

Sigtryg I do.

Sigurd I accept your offer then.

Voice Long live Sigurd, Earl of Orkney!

Thorstein Long live Sigurd, King of Dublin!

(*crowd cheers*)

Sigurd Well, my friend Thorstein, so far so good. I wonder what Gormlai will say to it.

Thorstein Gormlai has had three husbands – one Norse, two Irish. The Norse husband is dead. The Irish, though old, are still alive. She hates them both but most she hates Brian. She would like another Norseman under her wolfskin – not the least if he brought Brian's head with him.

Bishop Queen Gormlai –

Gormlai What is it now, my lord Bishop?

Bishop Queen Gormlai, I beg you to listen. These heathen Norsemen that you have sent for –

Gormlai What is this talk of heathen and Christian, Norseman and Irish,

Gael and Gall? Was not my first husband Norse – and a Christian? Was not my second Irish – and *you* know what he did, my lord Bishop. He plundered the shrine of St Patrick.

Bishop No more of that, Queen Gormlai.

Gormlai No more of that certainly; that was his great mistake. Your archbishop at Armagh never forgave him. But my third husband, Brian, his rival, *he* gave ten pounds of gold to Armagh.

Bishop He did – and God will reward him.

Gormlai He has been rewarded already. Where is Mael Seachlainn now? He was as good as Brian – and younger and stronger, I of all people know that – but Brian sits on his throne and he is now Brian's henchman.

Bishop They are united against the Norseman.

Gormlai United! United by fear. And it never was Brian who hated the Norsemen most. Did he not sail with them up the Shannon, looting?

Bishop There was a reason –

Gormlai There are always reasons. Fear, greed, envy, power-lust. I am tired of Irish kings, I have shared my bed with two of them.

Bishop So you would bring in the foreigners?

Gormlai The foreigners? Who are the foreigners? In this land of mists and cattle raids and bickerings, this land that is pinned together with thorn trees and still keeps falling apart, this land where you take one step and you sink in a bog or you take one glance at the sky and get lost in the clouds, was it not time for new blood, for men from the north and the east?

Bishop They burnt Clonmacnois.

Gormlai So did your Munstermen. But I grant you they burnt Clonmacnois. And they founded Waterford, Wexford, Anagassan, Limerick, Dublin. And they taught your metalworkers metal work and your boatbuilders how to build boats. Yes, and they even gave you coinage.

Bishop When you speak of the Irish, Queen Gormlai, why do you use the word 'you'?

Gormlai Because I no longer am one of you. I have some Norse blood and my first husband was Norse. I shall find another of his kind.

Bishop If you do that, let me warn you –

Gormlai Warn yourself, my lord Bishop. You are here under safe conduct but that does not excuse bad manners. You are not in Ireland now. This is the fort of Dublin.

77

Go; go back to Brian – Brian with his old man's dreams and his cold knotty fingers and his cunning. Go and join the rest of his toadies – his harpers, his poets, his jesters, his cup-bearers. I have seen his favourite wine-cup – all gold and garnets, but it leaks. I have seen the harp of his harper – of Irish oak, well-carved, there are wolfhounds carved on the pillar, but the instrument is unlucky.

Bishop Unlucky, Queen Gormlai?

Gormlai It was made to be played at a wake. It is not a harp for the young.
(*fade up harp, hold, and break off*)

Brian Why have you stopped?

Harper It stopped of itself, King Brian.

Poet How can a harp stop of itself?

Brian He means he is tired.

Poet He means he is idle, King Brian.

Brian Hold your tongue. I give you both too much licence.

Harper No, not tired nor idle. The harp stopped of itself.

Brian Silence! . . . Stopped of itself? . . . Who made that harp?

Harper But you know, King Brian!

Brian I asked you who made it.

Harper Colum the Dumb.

Poet He was not born dumb; the Danes cut his tongue out.

Harper Because he would not show them the monastery treasures.

Poet He made that harp to atone for his tongue.

Harper But when he had put in the last silver button and tuned the last string –

Poet He died!

Brian Stop talking! Who told you to talk? I do not feed you and clothe you to hear your tattle. As if I did not know about Colum the Dumb! Yes, he died.
(*pause*)
Well? Do what I keep you for. Make music, make poetry, work!

Poet Give me the lead.
(*snatch of harp*)

Harper Right?

Poet Right.
(*harp with recitation*)

Poet Once ere Brian took the throne
All this land was ache and moan;
Since he laid his peace on all
We can call our lives our own.

78

> Once our petty kings pursued
> Cattle raid and family feud;
> Since our High King put them down
> Through his crown is peace renewed.

Brian (*to self*) Mael Seachlainn? . . . Yes, I foxed him.

Poet Law and order east and west:
> Now a woman richly dressed
> Dares to walk the roads alone –
> None will scare her, none molest.

> Those who late were forced to eat
> Sloes and acorns live on meat;
> Those who slept in sty and ditch
> Now are rich and find it sweet.

> Like the eagle in his nest
> Brian lords it in the west;
> Like a green and towering tree
> It is he that tops the rest.

Brian (*to self*) No, not green, not green. . .

Poet When the vikings came ashore
> Brian waded in their gore;
> Let them come the more they would,
> Brian stood and slew the more.

> God is with him day and night,
> All His angels in their might
> Stand with flaming swords around,
> Stand their ground to –

Messenger King Brian! King Brian!
> (*poet and harp break off*)

Brian Where are you from, man?

Messenger Dublin: I went round the markets, heard the rumours. Sigtryg is back from Orkney.

Brian Yes?

Messenger Do not strike me, King Brian. Earl Sigurd of Orkney is coming. He took some persuading but Sigtryg persuaded him. He has sent out a summons to the viking world.

Brian (*more to self*): Sigurd of Orkney . . . a strong man, they tell me. . . If I were forty years younger, I – What are the three of you staring at? You! send for my son, Muragh.

Messenger At once, King Brian.

    Brian And my grandson Turlough with him. And you two leave me also. Take away your lies and your music! Leave me alone. I must think.

    Poet } God be with you, King Brian.
Harper }

    (*pause*)

    Brian Sixty years of wars . . . leading Munster against Leinster . . . one day against Mael Seachlainn, the next day with him . . . one day against the foreigner but the next – well, it's the fall of the dice. Mary, Queen of the Angels, forgive me; if I gambled, at least I won. The first High King of Ireland whose height was beyond challenge. But those who take the sword shall – Was this the hand that took it? The veins so swollen and knotted it might be the map of my history. Or the map of this whole doomed island. I need not go to the door to see what my country looks like. The bog like a purple running sore, the wood like a web of false intrigue, the wind like a whisper of foul intent, the hills like the graves of enormous hopes, the clouds like a tent of despair and death. Despair? Who is Earl Sigurd to make me despair! Let him come to Ireland if he wants to! Let him summon them all to Ireland! I shall receive them.

    (*viking horn*)

    Sigurd I, Sigurd, Earl of Orkney, having made a solemn undertaking with Sigtryg at present King of Dublin, hereby call on my brethren overseas to come with me to Dublin by Palm Sunday, there to defeat and slay Brian the High King of Ireland. And let me remind you there is still gold in Ireland. And fat cattle. And women. And let me remind you also: this war will be fought in the true manner of the vikings. There shall be no words of fear or of quarrel. All loot that is taken shall be brought to the pole. No sword shall be longer than an ell. No wound shall be bound till the same hour next day. No prisoners shall be taken. Nor, in your voyage to Dublin, shall your sails be furled for the wind. This is my summons – and these are the lands I send it to. Denmark!

    (*viking horn*)

  1st Dane I think I will go. What do you say? After all, last year we conquered England.

 2nd Dane Then, if you *must* cross the sea, why not go to England? It's nearer.

  1st Dane The loot is already shared out. Besides, the fighting is over there.

80

Sigurd Norway!
      (horn)
Norwegian So Sigurd is a Christian? A pity. I know, I too was baptised, like
    everyone else in this country. Herded like sheep to the font – but
    I never believed it. And it is the ruin of Norway. Look at us today –
    our land being grabbed by Danes and Swedes and all sorts. Ireland
    could not be worse. Yes, I think I will pay it a visit.
Sigurd The Faroes!
      (horn)
Faroe Man Hm? An invitation to Ireland! They say it is a land full of salmon
    and honey. And one thing about it.
Voice What?
Faroe Man It's a larger island than this. I have long been yearning for elbow
    room.
Sigurd Iceland!
      (horn)
Halgerda Come here, you Irish slut. Tell me about your country.
Slave Girl I have nothing to tell. I have forgotten it. Slaves have no memory,
    Halgerda.
Halgerda Is it true there is a woman there like me? Gormlai – is that her
    name?
Slave Girl Gormlai is a traitress – and a whore.
Halgerda I asked you: is she like me?
Slave Girl That is for you to judge.
      (slap)
    Thank you. She also had three husbands. But at least she did not
    murder them.
Halgerda Grim! If a slap will not cure you, I must take further measures.
Grim You called me, mistress?
Halgerda Take this girl out and flog her.
Slave Girl Oh no, no! Not again!
Grim This way, little jewel of Ireland.
Slave Girl No, no, no . . .
      (laughter from Halgerda)
Burner Why are you laughing Halgerda?
Halgerda Oh, the last of the burners! What cave have you been hiding in
    lately?
Burner You are not grateful, are you? You hated Njal. We burnt him.
Halgerda Gunnar my husband settled his debts with the sword.
Burner And we know what you did to Gunnar.

Halgerda You are not in a position to insult me in my house. When you burnt Njal and his household, you lit a fire that is not yet quenched. This land of ice is too hot for you.

Burner That is why I am leaving it.

Halgerda And a good riddance. But what do you want with me?

Burner I want a loan for my voyage.

Halgerda How far is your voyage?

Burner To Ireland.

Halgerda To Ireland? You! From all I have heard of King Brian, you cannot fight *him* with faggots. Why should I give you a loan?

Burner Because I did you a good turn.

Halgerda A good turn in an ill way. Tell me, do you know Ireland?

Burner I have been there once. Good looting.

Halgerda Did you see Queen Gormlai?

Burner I did. Even then she was plotting against Brian.

Halgerda They say she is tall and beautiful.

Burner Not as tall as you, Halgerda.

Halgerda Few women are.

Burner Nor as beautiful.

Halgerda You are doing well. Tell me more.

Burner She has eyes like blue ice, I think she has Norse blood. And what she wants, she will get. And once she has got it, she will want more.

Gormlai More, I tell you, more! You promise me Sigurd will be here by Palm Sunday, but he has not enough ships. There are thirty ships more lying west of Man this moment.

Sigtryg Whose ships are they, mother?

Gormlai Brodir's and Ospak's.

Sigtryg Those two brothers! Their help would be help.

Gormlai It is up to you to persuade them. Off to your ship! The Isle of Man is not far.

Etain I do not want him to go.

Gormlai *You* do not want him to go! And who are you to have any opinion?

Etain I am your son's wife.

Gormlai You are my son's enemy. I know you would wish King Brian to win.

Etain I am King Brian's daughter.

82

Gormlai You must choose between father and husband. It says in the Gospel –

Etain So *you* quote the Gospel now!

Sigtryg Be quiet! Mother, I shall go to Man. But how do I persuade Ospak and Brodir?

Gormlai As you did with Earl Sigurd. The throne of Dublin and my hand in marriage.

Sigtryg But Earl Sigurd –

Gormlai He need not know.

Sigtryg I will try then. But which of the brothers?

Gormlai Ospak has ten ships, Brodir twenty. Make your offer to Brodir.

Sigtryg But they say he is a heathen, a renegade – a man who was once a deacon.

Gormlai They say his hair is so long he can tuck it under his belt. What they say does not matter. Both those brothers are heathens.

Sigtryg Right. I will go to Brodir.

    (*viking horn, then sea-wash behind*)

Brodir Ha! ha! ha! ha! ha! So that is settled. I shall be in Dublin on Palm Sunday.

Sigtryg And you, Ospak?

Ospak No. I do not like double-dealing. Brian is a good king.

Brodir Then get back to your own ship. You are my brother no longer.

Ospak I never chose to be your brother, but let me warn you, Brodir. I, as you know, have the gift of foresight. I think you go to your death. And, as proof of this, this night in this ship you will see certain wonders. Or perhaps not see them – hear them and feel them. And in each of your twenty ships a man will be dead by morning.

Brodir You forget I have magic too.

Ospak You will need it, Brodir. And stop your ears with wax. Or else the noise may deafen you.

Brodir Deafen me?

    (*cross into wild din and behind*)

    Light! Light! Who has put out the light?

1st Viking Brodir! What is happening? Oh my face!

Brodir Shields! Take your shields, fend them off.

2nd Viking Thor god of battles! Their beaks are like iron. What are they?

Brodir Ravens, only ravens. Use your shields.

1st Viking Ravens, Brodir? Demons!

Brodir What do I care! Keep off there! Keep away, you fowls of hell!

(shouts and mixed noises, then a scream and falling body, then silence)
There goes my one man dead. You will answer for this, brother Ospak. And unless you answer me truly –

Ospak I will answer nothing till you pledge me peace.

(pause)

Well?

Brodir Right.

'As the meter meted and the teller told and the doomsman deemed and the givers gave –'

Ospak No, not now. Wait till nightfall.

Brodir Why?

Ospak I know you, Brodir. You never kill men by night. So I shall tell you then.

I shall tell you now. What happened last night foretold your doom. Those ravens which attacked you are the demons you put your faith in. When you all are dead in a short time from now in Ireland, it is those black demons that will drag you down to hell.

Brodir The raven is Odin's bird.

Ospak True. Let Odin protect you then.

Brodir He is your god too.

Ospak No longer. I go to the god you forsook.

Brodir You will take baptism?

Ospak Yes.

Brodir Then I shall not see you in Ireland.

Ospak You *will* see me in Ireland. But in the ranks of King Brian. No, don't draw your sword. Remember your pledge. Besides, Brodir, it is night still.

Brodir Night? Yes, black as a raven. Never mind, I will pray to the god of ravens. And you, you can pray to the man on the naked tree. But you do not know those prayers yet – the prayers that I have forgotten. They are more fit for old men like Brian. They will not get you to Valhalla.

Brian Deus meus adiuva me.

Bishop Salus tua, Domine, sit semper nobiscum.

Brian Have mercy upon us, O God the Father Almighty.

Bishop O beginning of all things,

Brian O true knowledge,

Bishop O morning star,

84

Brian   O tree of life,

Bishop   O lily of the valleys,

Brian   O lion,

Bishop   O eagle,

Brian   O Christ crucified!

Bishop   Have mercy upon us.

Brian   Have mercy upon us.

Slave Girl   Mary, mother of God, mother of the golden light, Mary greatest of Marys, heal the weals on my back, I cannot sleep for the pain of them. And Mary queen of the angels, fountain of the gardens, star of the sea, I pray you to raise the waves of the sea and sink all the ships of the vikings before they make land in my country. But if they should reach my country, hear the prayer of a slave girl in Iceland far from her home; O Mary queen of the heavens, if those long evil ships with the round shields on their gunwales and the dragons' heads on their prows should come to the mouth of the Liffey –

Old Woman   There child, what did I tell you! The dragons are back from the north, they are hungry. Look how the sun glints on the shields on the gunwales. I have seen them often before, time and again I have seen them, but never so many as this; the whole of the bay is afroth with them. If I were King Brian I would hide in the woods. I am as old as he is, older maybe but I've no wish to die. He rests his head on a pillow of feathers, I have not even a pillow of chaff; for all that I sleep the sounder. And I sleep as sound as Queen Gormlai for all her gold and her lovers. These great folk are all the same. They do no good to us. They do no good to themselves. Gormlai! If I were her husband I would take my shield to bed with me.

Gormlai   Earl Sigurd, I welcome you to Dublin. You look as my son described you.

Sigurd   Thank you, Queen Gormlai. You look more than he described you.

Gormlai   More what?

Sigurd   Beautiful. Fierce.

Gormlai   Good. Bring us some wine there.

So you could not describe me, Sigtryg!

85

Sigtryg Who could, mother, who could?

Gormlai Yes. I am not dead yet.

You eat sucking pig, Earl Sigurd?

Sigurd When I can get it, Queen Gormlai.

Gormlai I have killed a hundred for supper. It is an Irish delicacy.

Sigurd Ireland, I think, must be full of delicacies.

Gormlai Ireland is full of good things – and bad things. When I lived with Brian – may he still sleep uneasy! – in Kincora, around our house was a great earth dyke with crab-apple trees and ash trees. And the wind moaned in those trees while Brian moaned beside me. That old man talks in his sleep; the memories he has are too many and black.

Etain It is not true. I will not listen –

Gormlai Who asked you to?

Etain Sigtryg! Tell her –

Sigtryg My mother should know.

Etain King Brian has many memories but they are not black, they are golden.

Sigurd So you praise King Brian?

Etain He is my father.

Sigurd Your father! Whom then do you want to win?

Etain My father. I will go now.

Gormlai Yes, Etain, go to your work-basket. Try a little embroidery. Why not embroider a shroud? That would be daughterly of you.

(*laughter from crowd*)

Sigurd A girl of spirit.

Gormlai You think so? Well, what was I saying? Yes, my life in Kincora away out there in the west. Round our house was a dyke and beyond that dyke was a bog, with stumps of grey bog-oak in it like the broken bones of giants. One night when I could not sleep I put on a thick woollen cloak and went to the edge of that bog and there was a will-o'-the-wisp. And I called to him 'What is your life?' You know what he answered?

Sigurd So he answered?

Gormlai He answered by action; he vanished. And that, I thought, is the life of the people in Ireland. They dart here and there, they flicker and fade in the bogs – but for me, I want something more solid. That is why I sent for you. Was I right, Sigurd?

Sigurd I suppose I am more solid than a will-o'-the-wisp.

(*laughter*)

Gormlai What would you say was the difference between your people and the Irish?

Sigurd I think there are many differences. We have better aims. We build better ships. We talk less.

Gormlai And you are more solid? Both in body and spirit. You are better fighters? And better lovers?

Sigurd That you must judge for yourself, Queen Gormlai.

Gormlai I think you will win this battle.

Sigurd I think so too – but what will be will be.

Gormlai What day is it set for?

Sigurd I have left that to Brodir.

Gormlai Why to Brodir?

Sigurd He practises divination.

Gormlai Divination! I should not have thought you cared for that. Well, has he done his divining?

Sigurd No, he would have told me. But I will encourage him. Brodir!

Gormlai Why, is he here?

Sigurd Here he comes.

Gormlai So his hair *is* as long as they say.

Brodir Earl Sigurd?

Sigurd It is time you did your divining.

Brodir I have done so, Earl Sigurd.

Sigurd Then why did you not tell me?

Brodir Ill news keeps.

Sigurd Go on.

Brodir If we fight before Good Friday, all of us shall fall.

Sigurd Then we do not fight before Good Friday.

Brodir If we fight on Good Friday, Brian shall fall.

Gormlai Good. Bring us more wine there!

Brodir Brian shall fall – but he will win.

Gormlai I do not believe you. If Brian falls, the rest of them will vanish like will-o'-the-wisps.

Sigurd Will-o'-the-wisps have a trick of reappearing.

Gormlai *You* don't believe him, do you?

Sigurd Maybe I do, maybe not. No matter; we fight on Good Friday.

Gormlai Sigurd, you disappoint me. A man of your strength should not meddle with omens.

Brodir I think there will be more omens. Once Good Friday is with us. And good will be the wrong word.

　　　(*witch-weaving music*)

87

1st Caithness Man Can you see in?

2nd Caithness Man No. Let me get on your shoulders.

1st C. Man I'd rather we went. There's something wrong about this,

2nd C. Man What's wrong? They are only weaving. There are plenty of looms in Caithness.

1st C. Man Aye, but this barn they are weaving in – this barn was not here yesterday.

2nd C. Man Are you sure?

1st C. Man I live half a mile from here. There is no such barn on this moor.

2nd C. Man Come, let me get on your shoulders. That's it. Now raise yourself. Just a little higher and I'll get my eye to the window slit. St Michael and All Angels! Odin, Thor and Freya!

1st C. Man What is it?

2nd C. Man Women – but they are not women. The light is dim but they are not women. And that loom, it's dripping with blood. Listen! Now they're singing.

The Fates This is our warp   this is our woof,
　　　The hot guts of heroes;
　　We weave we sisters   the sorrowful tale
　　　Of lives to be lost.

　　In this dark morning   we weave the doom
　　　Of bold men in battle
　　On a far shore   on this evil Friday
　　　We weave and we weave . . .
　　　(*fade out loom music, fade up Brian*)

Brian Hos omnes invoco in auxilium meum.

Bishop Forty saints in Glendalough.

Brian Per Jesum.

Bishop Four thousand monks with the grace of God in Bangor.

Brian Per Jesum.

Bishop Twelve youths who went with Columcille on pilgrimage to Alba.

Brian Per Jesum.

Bishop The hermit found by Brendan in the Land of Promise.

Brian Per Jesum.

Bishop Seven holy bishops of the Church of the Yew Wood.

Brian Per Jesum.

Bishop Seven holy bishops of Tuam in Galway.

Brian Per Jesum.

88

Bishop Seven holy bishops of Donaghmore in Leitrim.

Brian Per Jesum.

Bishop Seven holy bishops of Donaghmore in Limerick.

Brian Per Jesum.

Bishop Seven holy bishops of –

Muragh Father!

Brian Muragh! You should not enter this chapel like that. Take off your helmet.

Muragh I am sorry, father, but time runs on. It will be dawn soon. They are all waiting for their orders.

Brian One moment.

O warrior Michael help me in the hour of my departing.

Bishop Amen.

Muragh Why that prayer, father?

Brian This night I heard the banshee. Today is my last. And, as I told you, I shall spend it in prayer.

Muragh Here?

Brian On the fringe of the battle. They must set up my tent where I know what goes on. In Tomar's Wood. I will have the lad Teigue there with me; he will be company enough. And you, Muragh, the battle is yours. If you fall, the command goes to Turlough.

Muragh Turlough is too young.

Brian He too has my blood in his veins. What my son can do, my grandson can do. Goodbye, my lord Bishop; I go to my conference.

Bishop God be with you, King Brian.

Brian And with you too. And with all of us. Muragh, I am ready.

Muragh It is time. I dare say Sigurd is holding his conference already. Those vikings are early birds.

Brian The early bird is the one the worms eat first. God forgive me, I should not joke on Good Friday. Where is my crown?

Muragh You are wearing it.

Brian Ha! It is time I died. Is Mael Seachlainn up?

Muragh They are all up.

Brian And my harper too?

Muragh And your harper.

Brian He too may fight if he wants to. I have not allowed it before but I shall not need him again. Let him play for me once before it starts. But, before that, some different music. Let them sound the handbells. Let my army know I am coming. Today will decide everything.

(montage of hand bells and fade slowly)

Sigurd That is all, fellow vikings. Today will decide everything.

Brodir Earl Sigurd?

Sigurd Yes, Brodir?

Brodir Two miles, I think, is too wide a front.

Sigurd I do not think so. Is it two miles, Maelmordha? This is your country.

Maelmordha To Clontarf is more than two miles. It would be two miles between the Tolka and the Liffey.

Brodir And you're posting me by the Tolka two miles from Dublin?

Sigurd Would you rather stay inside with Sigtryg?

Brodir If that is an insult I ignore it. Everyone knows how I fight. But the whole of that ground is wet; we should not spread out too much.

Sigurd If we do not, they can outflank us and cut off our ships.

Maelmordha That is true, that is just what they would do. We Irish have a saying: a viking without his ship is like an ox that's been hobbled.

Brodir We vikings have another saying: when an Irishman changes sides –

Maelmordha Norsemen change sides too. I heard you have a brother, Brodir.

Brodir By Thor and his hammer –

Sigurd Silence! Norsemen or Irish, we are all against Brian.

Maelmordha Yes, we are all against Brian. In Leinster we do not like Munstermen.

Sigurd I am grateful to you, Maelmordha, and all your Leinstermen with you. And let us have no more bickering. My orders stand: Brodir on the right by the Tolka, myself in the centre with Maelmordha on my left, and left of him again the Norseman from Dublin.

Brodir The bridge will be handy if they run.

Thorstein But Sigtryg may not open the gate to them.

Voice As a Dublin Norseman I resent that.

Thorstein On your own behalf or on Sigtryg's?

Sigurd Thorstein, your tongue is too rough.

Thorstein It's a way we have in Iceland. Maybe it comes from having no kings or earls there.

Brodir Where will Ospak be stationed?

Sigurd How should I know? Can I read the mind of King Brian?

Brian And right of Mael Seachlainn comes Ospak. Ospak, you hold our right flank. That is all clear then? From left to right this is our order.

My son Muragh, in command of the whole army. Next my grandson, Turlough. Then the main forces of Munster. Then Mael Seachlainn, we have often fought together.

Mael Seachlainn Sometimes beside each other, sometimes against each other.

Brian What was that, Mael Seachlainn?

Mael S. I said that you and I were like brother and brother.

Ospak That proves nothing.

Brian Ospak! Where was I? Yes, with Mael Seachlainn. Ah, yes, on his right the Connaughtmen and right of them, on the flank by the Liffey, Ospak. Now I shall shake you each by the hand. When you leave this tent, I shall not see you again.

Muragh Do not speak like that, father. I have placed a strong guard round this tent, they will stand here shield to shield till the battle is over. Is that not so, Captain of the Guard?

Captain It is indeed, Prince Muragh. Why would the King be afraid –

Brian The King be afraid! Come here, oaf!

Captain I only meant afraid we would desert. We will stand round this tent like dolmens on the hillsides. We will stand like the Rock of Cashel –

Brian You need not go on. You will stand.

Captain Stand is the word. Stand like the cliffs of Moher. Stand like –

Brian Have you been drinking?

Captain No. I will drink tonight.

Brian At my wake, you mean. Give me your hand. . . . Yes, you have a grip. Goodbye.

Muragh To your post, Captain of the Guard.

Brian Ospak, your hand. I am glad you are with us.

Ospak I am glad, King Brian, I have learnt the true faith. And today, if I meet my brother Brodir –

Brian I leave that to you. Goodbye.
   Mael Seachlainn! Where are you?

Mael S. But I'm here.

Brian My sight must be going. I am old.

Mael S. I am old too. Sixty-five.

Brian That is nothing. And yet I beat you at times.

Mael S. I beat you at times too.

Brian Still I won in the end. Who is the High King now?

Mael S. You know why I yielded –

Brian Let bygones be bygones. You were High King fourteen years –

Mael S. Nineteen.

Brian You are right. It is I have been High King fourteen. And now for some twelve hours more.

Mael S. Do not say that, Brian.

Brian Goodbye, Mael Seachlainn.

Mael S. Goodbye, Brian. God be with you.

Brian Muragh!

Muragh Father?

Brian I will not delay you. You must fight your battle – my battle. Remember that some of these vikings wear chain-mail.

Muragh I have met vikings before, father. Besides, it is only their leaders.

Brian You will be meeting their leaders. Well, God be with you. Goodbye, son.

Muragh Goodbye, father. I will do what I can.

Brian Turlough!

Turlough Grandfather!

Brian None of them believe me, do they?

Turlough When you say what?

Brian When I say today is my last.

Turlough I believe you. I heard the banshee too.

Brian *You* heard! That is not good.

Turlough Muragh heard it too.

Brian Muragh too?... So much for my family. But there's one missing. My daughter. Why is Etain not here to say goodbye to me?

Turlough She is in Dublin. With Sigtryg.

Brian Ah, yes, of course. And with Gormlai?

Turlough And with Gormlai.

Brian And they threw her down from the window and the dogs devoured her carcase. Gormlai! May she meet the fate of Jezebel!

Turlough Grandfather, goodbye. The battle will be starting.

Brian The battle? To be sure. But I fear I shall not see it. My eyes are misting over. It is not so light as it was. Teigue!

Teigue King Brian?

Brian Hold back the flap of the tent there. It must be dawn by now. Is it dawn, Turlough?

Turlough It is.

Brian Are you holding back the flap of the tent?

Teigue I am so.

Brian How is the sky?

Teigue Red. The shepherd's warning.

Brian The shepherd's? Ha, ha, ha! Yes, I can see a red glow. Still it's not
so light as it was. Turlough!

(*pause*)

Turlough, answer.

Teigue King Brian, he went. He was late.

Brian Call him back. No. He is needed over there on the left. Where is
my harper?

Harper Here, King Brian.

Brian And my poet?

Poet Here too.

Brian Good. I want a new piece – a last piece. I want – what do they call
it – a swansong.

Poet Give me the lead.

(*snatch of harp*)

Harper Right?

Poet Right.

(*harp with voice*)

Poet In his tent sits Brian blind,
Visions blazing in his mind,
Lesser men may fight and see,
Only he must stay behind.

To the east towards Dublin Bay
Stand the vikings in array,
Great fair men with eyes of blue –
Who knows who will win the day?

To the east the longships ride,
Painted dragons side by side;
From Clontarf to Liffey bank
Rank on rank the hosts abide.

On our left by Tolka weir
Muragh waits and twirls his spear,
Next him Turlough –

Brian Stop!

(*voice and harp break off*)

Brian Muragh! Turlough! Why are you two not with them?

Harper But, King Brian –

Brian Give me that harp.

Poet It was your order that –
(*effect of smashing harp*)
Brian There! This is no day for music. Only for prayer – and bloodshed.
Off with you two to the battle.
Poet God be with you, King Brian.
Harper God be with you, King Brian.
(*pause*)
Brian Teigue, have you the psalter?
Teigue The psalter?
Brian The great book in the golden case. You will have to read it aloud
to me. But first spread the wolfskin on the ground.
Teigue It is spread already. At your feet.
Brian Good. Help me down to kneel on it. A hundred and fifty psalms
there are. That might see out the battle. Thank you, Teigue. How
is the weather?
Teigue Sharp. Very sharp.
Brian Sharp? To be sure. Sharp as nails.
Right. Psalm One.
Teigue 'Blessed is the man that walketh not in the counsel of the ungodly;
nor standeth in the way of sinners; nor sitteth in the seat of the
scornful. . .'
Sigurd Good! Unfurl my banner!
Thorstein We know about that banner. Everyone dies who carries it.
Sigurd True – but a fine piece of needlework.
My mother made it. She was Irish.
There! Look at it.
Voices (*cheering*) The raven! The raven!
(*horns and handbells*)
Old Woman Look, man, look! They're swarming like fleas in a sheepskin.
We'll have a grand view from here. They'll be fighting any
moment now.
Ploughman Let them fight! I have this field to plough. What are you doing
here anyway?
Old Woman You're late for ploughing – this is April. I've come to see the sport.
There'll be great killing today.
Ploughman I have a brother down there. My twin – but a born fool. They've
put him to guard King Brian. He couldn't guard these oxen here!
Old Woman Look, can't you! That big man by the banner.
Sigurd (*calling*) Brodir, can you hear me!
Brodir (*calling*) Earl Sigurd?

94

Sigurd   The honour is yours. Begin.

Brodir   Thank you, Earl Sigurd.

Sound the war-horn.

(*challenge on horn*)

Old Woman   Who's that fellow just over the stream there stepping forward?
With long black hair flowing down under his helmet.

Brodir   Muragh, son of Brian! Do you hear me?

Muragh   I hear you, Brodir. Come and meet me.

Brodir   I am coming, Muragh.

Draw your swords.

(*up battle music, music with effects and shouting, and behind*)

Maelmordha   Come on, Leinstermen! Down with those Munster upstarts!

(*up music, then quickly to distance behind*)

Gormlai   There goes my brother. Look, the Irish are breaking.

Sigtryg   Brodir is doing well too. It is too far to see who is who but away
over there to the north you can see the flow of the armies. And
that flow is clearly westward; the Irish are giving ground fast.
Brodir and Sigurd – which of them would you choose, mother?

Gormlai   Whichever of them survives. Yes, Brodir is driving back Muragh.

Etain   Look a little nearer. Your Dublin vikings are not finding it easy.

Gormlai   Etain! Back to your work-basket.

Sigtryg   Or else hold your tongue.

Etain   Sigurd too is not finding it so easy –

Sigtryg   Etain, speaking as your husband and also as Sigurd's friend –

Etain   How dare you speak as my husband? Still less as Sigurd's friend!
If you are his friend, what are you doing here? Skulking in Dublin,
perched on this watch-tower with the women –

Gormlai   (*laughs*) A hit, Etain, a hit! But stop squabbling. You see what's
happening? Away over there, towards the Tolka, Brodir has
broken them. And Leinster has broken Munster. The battle is
boiling like a broth of leeks. But it's all but over, all but over.

(*up music and effects and behind*)

Muragh   Stand, you weaklings! What's wrong with you!

Brodir   Freya, goddess of battles! Look at them running!

Mael S.   Michael, bring your angels or we're lost!

Thorstein   Ha, Sigurd! Men will write verse about this.

(*fade out music and effects*)

Skald   By the weir of the Tolka   warriors gathered
In evil April   on Irish marshland
Gael against Gall   on a grey morning

95

Close to Clontarf   clamped in death-grip
Havoc disturbed   the heron's fishing,
On Dublin's gates   they doubled the bars,
Sigtryg the coward   crouched behind them.
Then did Earl Sigurd   scythe the warfield,
The wizard Brodir   whittle their spearshafts,
Thorstein of Iceland   thrive in the swordplay.
Against them mustered   Muragh and Turlough
Shin deep in water   shining with bloodlust
Behind them Brian   bowed with years
Knelt in his tent   in Tomar's Wood.

(fade up distant battle effects and behind)

Teigue Here beginneth the twenty-second psalm.

My God, my God, why hast thou forsaken me?

Why art thou so far from helping me, and from the words of my roaring?

Brian Roaring? *I* am not roaring. But my knees feel the damp of the ground under this wolf-skin.

Teigue Our fathers trusted in thee; they trusted and thou didst deliver them. They cried unto thee and were delivered; they trusted in thee and were not confounded.

(cross-fade Teigue into foreground battle music)

Sigurd Resting, Thorstein?

Thorstein I'm reading a face, Earl Sigurd.

Sigurd Whose face?

Thorstein That one at my feet. I have just killed him. A moment ago he looked angry; now he looks only surprised.

Sigurd The dead look often surprised. But back to business, Thorstein. This is a great day for Orkney.

Thorstein A great day for Iceland too. A pity the people at home there cannot see how the battle goes.

Sigurd In Iceland! They'd need long sight.

(fade out music and effects)

Slave Girl Here is your jewel box, Halgerda.

Halgerda Good. Now what shall I choose? See this silver tortoise brooch? Made by the best silversmith in Norway. And this bracelet? It came from Constantinople. By the way, I want my red dress from the chest.

Slave Girl I will fetch it. Are you expecting guests?

Halgerda No; today I dress for myself. Today is a great day.

96

Slave Girl Why?

Halgerda Haven't you heard – even a slave must have heard – today is the day they fixed for the battle. In your country, hundreds of miles to the south. That red dress, I wore it the day my husband Gunnar came wooing me. It is also red for blood.

Slave Girl Whose blood?

Halgerda That of your people. They have no chance, you poor wretch.

Slave Girl That is what you say.

Halgerda Ha! Don't stare at me like that; I can outstare the world. Go and fetch me that dress and the bodice that goes with it.

(*fade up battle music or effects, but keep distant behind*)

Teigue Here beginneth the sixty-ninth psalm.

'Save me, O God, for the waters are come in unto my soul. I sink in deep mire where there is no standing; I am come into deep waters where the floods overflow me. I am weary of my crying, I am dry in the throat; while I wait for my God my eyes fail me.'

(*up battle music and effects and behind*)

Muragh Brodir! Brodir you renegade! So it was not as easy as you thought! Yes, Brodir, the tide has turned. Come on, Brodir, and meet me! Ha! I might have guessed it.

(*fade out music and effects*)

Skald
Now does Brodir	battered by Muragh
Take to his heels,	hide in a thorncopse;
Muragh's long sword	minces the remnant,
On his right young Turlough	ramps like a lion.
Yet does not Sigurd	yield to their onset,
Not for nothing	noted in Orkney;
Stout as an oak	he stands in the centre,
Rallies the vikings	raises his war-cry

Sigurd Christ and Valhalla!

(*up battle music and effects and behind*)

Thorstein Earl Sigurd, your banner has fallen.

Sigurd Pick it up then. Who slew the bearer?

Thorstein Turlough, grandson of Brian. But to all who bear it that banner is death. I will not pick it up, Earl Sigurd.

Sigurd Hrafn the Red, bear you the banner.

Hrafn Bear your own devil yourself!

Sigurd Hm, so that is your tone now? Well, I suppose, the beggar must bear his own bag. I will take it from its staff and wear it like a cloak.

97

D

Come, you old raven, in honour to my mother and her needle –
There, let us cut our way through them.

Thorstein Inland? Away from the sea?

Sigurd What does it matter? Every man's last fight is a defeat.
Coming, Thorstein?

Thorstein I'm coming.

(up battle music, then fade effects to distance behind)

Teigue Here beginneth the hundred and twenty-fourth psalm. 'If it had
not been the Lord who was on our side, if it had not been the Lord
who was on our side when men rose up against us –

Brian One moment, Teigue. Open the flap of the tent and see how the
day goes.
(to self) If it had not been the Lord who was on my side . . . when I
was young and I hid in the woods in North Munster, when I beat
the foreigners at Limerick, when my brother Mahon was
murdered –

Teigue King Brian! King Brian! We have won!

Brian Already?

Teigue The vikings are running like hares. There are only a few here and
there still holding.

Brian God be praised – but what will follow will follow. Go on with
your reading now, Teigue.

Teigue 'If it had not been the Lord who was on our side when men rose
up against us, then they had swallowed us up quick when their
wrath was kindled against us. Then the waters had overwhelmed
us, the stream had gone over our soul. . . '

1st Guard Captain!

Captain What is it?

1st Guard The battle is over. What about loot?

Captain Our orders were to stay here and protect the King.

1st Guard Sure he needs no protecting now.

2nd Guard That's true enough.

3rd Guard True enough.

1st Guard If we wait till we're relieved, the pickings will be gone. I could do
with a nice viking helmet –

2nd Guard Or one of their axes maybe.

Captain Yes, their arms are better than ours. But do you think he'd notice?

1st Guard Who? The King? Sure he won't, he's at his prayers.

2nd Guard Authorise us, Captain, authorise us.

Captain Well now. . .

98

1st Guard They say some of those vikings wear gold rings on their arms. Think what you'd get for one in ale.

Captain You're right. A power of ale. Very good, lads, let's go!
(*cheering of guards and fade; effects distant behind*)

Old Woman Now isn't that a grand sight? But they're trying to cross the Tolka, I hope they don't come up here.

Ploughman Why would they come up here? They'll be veering off there to the bay. Well, I've some furrows more to plough before the light fails.

Old Woman Wait now, wait, man; look at that.

Ploughman What?

Old Woman A small group of foreigners yonder, they've cut their way through, they're making for Tomar's Wood.

Ploughman Tomar's Wood? That's where King Brian is.

Old Woman Is it now? With your brother guarding him.

Ploughman Ach, my brother! With his head as wooden as this plough. I wouldn't care about *him*.

Old Woman Look, man, they're entering the wood now.

Sigurd So you've joined us again, Brodir.

Brodir And why not, Earl Sigurd?

Sigurd I thought you had had your fill.

Brodir I lost the head of my axe. I could not fight Muragh with the shaft.

Thorstein Whose axe is that then?

Sigurd Hsh. See that tent – further on in the wood there? Listen!

Thorstein Voices.

Sigurd Brodir, now you are armed again – and not so tired as the rest of us, perhaps you will go ahead and find who is there in that tent?

Thorstein I will go with him.

Sigurd Good.

Teigue Here beginneth the hundred and thirtieth –

Brian No, Teigue, that is enough. Besides, you are losing your voice. Keep quiet now; I have someone to talk to.

Tibi soli peccavi et omne malum coram te feci. Peccavi et multiplicata sunt peccata mea super numerum harene maris – more than the sands of the sea – et non sum dignus videre altitudinem celi – no, not worthy, not worthy – prae multitudine peccatorum meorum.

Thorstein A priest!

Brodir In a crown?!

99

Brian Who's there?

Brodir Your enemies, Brian. Stand up if you want to.

Brian No, I will meet my death kneeling.

Thorstein Wait, Brodir –

Brodir Back! Thorstein! Give me room!

Brian Christus adjuva me.

    (*effect*)

Thorstein You should not have done that.

Brodir Should not have! Let the whole world know that Brodir killed Brian.

    (*up music, then behind*)

Skald Thus falls Brian	Brodir boasts;
Brodir Here lies Brian	High King of Ireland!
Skald No victory for that	the vikings gain.
Few are they now,	and far from the sea.
Longsighted Sigurd	looks to the east
Shading his eyes –	his ships are distant;
His line of retreat	is lost to the Irish
And here come the Irish	hot for the kill,
Muragh and Turlough	mad for vengeance;
Muragh swabs	the sweat from his eyes
And looks for Brodir	to left and right
But Brodir himself	breaks to the front
And faces Muragh –	
Brodir Muragh, son of Brian!	I have killed your father.
What is your answer?	

Muragh This is my answer.

    (*up music and effects of single combat*)

Thorstein Lay on, Brodir!

Turlough Watch his axe!

Thorstein Brodir, keep your shield up!

Turlough Muragh!

    (*crash*)

    Well done, Muragh.

Sigurd Get your breath again, Muragh. I'm ready when you are.

Muragh You are the Earl?

Sigurd I am the Earl – and this is my standard. My mother made it; she was Irish.

Muragh Yes, the work in it looks Irish. I'm ready, Sigurd.

Sigurd Will you fight without shields?

100

(effect of shield dropping)
Muragh   There!
          (effect of shield dropping)
Sigurd   There! Now Muragh, son of Brian!
          (up single combat music and behind)
Skald   Now it is come   combat between them
       Sigurd and Muragh   shieldless both –
Turlough   Muragh!
Thorstein   Sigurd!
Skald   mad with war-hate,
       The odds are on Orkney –
Turlough   Ireland!
Thorstein   Orkney!
Skald   Sigurd's sword   slips in his fingers
       Muragh snatches   the moment of luck,
       Pierces his guard,   the point goes home,
       But as Sigurd totters,   he too takes aim,
       With flagging strength   flails at the neck,
       This time for Muragh   a mortal blow,
       So both men fall   by friends regretted –
Turlough   Woe in Ireland!
Thorstein   Wonder in Orkney!
          (fade out music)
Hareck   Yonder! Do you see yonder?
Attendant   What, Hareck?
Hareck   Those men on horseback.
Attendant   I see no such thing. No men. No horses –
Hareck   It is the Earl. I know by his riding.
Attendant   You are mad, man. Earl Sigurd today is fighting in Ireland. How
       could he be here in Orkney?
Hareck   It is Earl Sigurd, I tell you. Or can this mean, does it mean – ?
          (percussion effect, then battle music behind)
Turlough   What this means is: the vikings are beaten. Sigurd is dead, there
       is no more resistance. After them, fast as you can! After, after,
       after, after, after!
          (rout music and behind)
Skald   Now runs Gall,   Gael pursues him
       Hacking his hams   hounding him south
       To the brimming Liffey   the bridge to Dublin
       But the town stands closed,   the two-faced merchants

Gather in counsel,   call on Gormlai,
Gormlai and Sigtryg   to salve their conscience.
    (*fade out rout music*)

Sigtryg You are asking me, you merchants of Dublin –

Gormlai I will speak, Sigtryg; from this day on, my son, no one in Ireland respects you.

Etain No one anywhere.

Gormlai Etain!

Merchants of Dublin, you want my advice. Are we to open the gates to your fellows? Before I answer, there is something I must know. Is there anyone here from the battlefield?

Burner I am.

Gormlai Oh you? One of the Burners from Iceland! How did you get into Dublin?

Burner I swam the Liffey and found a gap in the fence.

Gormlai You Burners would find a gap in anything. No matter, I want some news. Is Earl Sigurd still alive?

Burner He is dead.

Gormlai And Brodir?

Burner Dead too.

Etain So there you have it, Queen Gormlai!

Gormlai Yes, as you say, there I have it. Either would have suited me. *And* made a good king of Dublin. Unlike my son here, your husband.

Sigtryg Mother, I –

Gormlai Merchants of Dublin! I can read your minds like a book – a book with sorry pictures in the margin. You do not want me to open the gates to your kinsmen. Well, nor do I; I have no love for runaways. Let the Irish hound them as they will.
    (*up rout music and behind*)

Turlough After them! Give them no quarter! Kill every man of them – God of Hosts! What are *you* doing?

Thorstein Tying my shoe.

Turlough Why don't you run like the others?

Thorstein Turlough, I'm tying my shoe. Besides, I live in Iceland. However fast I might run, I shouldn't get home tonight.
    (*long laugh from Turlough*)

Turlough All right. You may go. Good luck to you.
    (*up rout music and behind*)

Skald Now runs Gall,   Gael pursues him
North to the woeful   weir of Clontarf;

102

With blood they tarnish	Tolka's waters,
Foothold is faulty,	few get over,
Slipping in slime	they are slain in hundreds,
Food for fish	they falter and sink,
As they enter the water	the Irish strike them,
Sword on the flanks	flail on the neck
Spear in the kidneys,	they spit and vanish –
Vengeance for Brian,	victory for Turlough,
Brian is murdered,	Muragh his son
Dead in the turmoil,	Turlough his grandson –
Here he comes now	the High King's heir –
Here he comes now	to harass the vikings,
To clinch the conflict,	cap the story,
The young man Turlough	yearning for vengeance.

                (*music and effects change to water theme*)

Turlough You there!

Captain of Guard Is it me?

Turlough Haven't I seen you before?

Captain No, Prince Turlough.

Turlough Then how do you know me? You are the man who deserted his post.

Captain No, it was my twin.

Turlough You have a twin? I suppose that could be true.

Captain It is. And he didn't want to leave his post. It was the others persuaded him. Loot, they kept saying, there'll be loot – grand viking helmets and axes and golden arm rings would buy you a twelve months' drinking.

Turlough So you can't even lie properly! How would you know what they said to your twin? Kneel down and say your prayers, man.

Captain Oh no, Prince Turlough, no! I didn't mean to, I didn't.

Turlough Kneel down – and make them short.

                (*lose music, hold effects behind in distance*)

Old Woman Ploughman, there's something strange going on now.

Ploughman Leave me alone. I must plough my last furrow.

Old Woman There's a man down there – he looks somehow familiar – and he's kneeling on the bank of the Tolka.

Ploughman – Oh, so he's gone.

Kneeling . . . seems to be praying. But who would that be standing over him – with a sword in his hand – but he's raising it. Mother of God!

103

(scream, distant)

The murdering villain! To kill a man when he's praying. But look, that serves him right. Overbalanced as he struck him and fell himself in the Tolka – may the devil drag him down and drown him. Floundering about in the water now – can't find his feet, it's carrying him down towards the weir. There, he's hit his head on a post – he's under, will he come up again. . . Will he come up again? . . . No, lost in the lather and pother. . . No, he's gone for good now. . . Well, whoever he was, there's some justice in heaven.

(cross-effects into solo harp – a snatch of a lament – then silence)

Poet   How does it compare, harper?

Harper   It's not like the one the king broke. But it will do. Are you ready?

Poet   Ready.

(harp and voice)

Poet   Now Good Friday's light is spent,
Brian murdered in his tent,
Muragh dead and Turlough dead –
Rough and red the way they went.

Shattered lies the viking host;
Deeds we wrought of which to boast,
Yet in Ireland never an eye
Can be dry from coast to coast.

Now that Brian to heaven is gone,
His two servants linger on,
He the harper, I the bard,
Hard we find it –

Mael S.   Hard you find it?

Harper   King Mael Seachlainn!

Mael S.   You are my servants now. I am taking you on.

Poet   We thank you for that.

Mael S.   And there is something else I am taking on – or back. The High Kingship of Ireland. But before I am crowned yet again, I will bury Brian at Armagh. It will be the greatest funeral ever yet seen in Ireland.

(to self) Yes, he did me much wrong but . . . it will be the finest funeral.

(fade up crowd of women lamenting)

Crowd Ochone! Ochone!

Old Woman Why do you do that?

(*lament breaks off*)

Woman We are mourning.

Old Woman Mourning? Aha! They pay you for it.

Woman I know they pay us – but these tears are tears. May he have it easy on the road to heaven. May the veils of fire and of ice that clash at the gate stand still for him. May he pass through the seven crystal walls and hear the birds that sing there.

Women Ochone! Ochone!

Old Woman So you're weeping for Brian? The last time I wept was for the murrain on the cattle. That makes more sense.

Woman Who are you? Where do you come from?

Old Woman Dublin.

Woman Dublin.

Old Woman On my two feet. But I wouldn't weep for his death; I am just here for the spectacle. Great folk give us little else but, when they get married or die, they give us a grand show. Or even when they are born; I know that well.

Woman Why?

Old Woman I have been a midwife in the houses of kings – great big white-washed houses with fires half the length of the hall and skins not only to sit on but skins to wrap round your feet – and the roof so high you would hardly see the swallows in the rafters.

Woman So you are a midwife?

Old Woman I was, I got tired of the business. There are too many people born anyway. No, a birth is nothing to a death.

Woman Mary and the saints protect us! You had best move on, strange woman.

Old Woman I am moving on but let me tell you this. You are mourning for Brian and thanking God for his victory. Is that so? Thanking God for it!

Woman We are thanking God indeed. That battle has settled matters.

Old Woman That battle has settled nothing. Ask the people who know. Just ask the big people who know.

Bishop You see this crozier in my hand? I held it in my hand on the morning of Good Friday. When I blessed King Brian before he went to the battle. And the blessing I gave him and the hopes we all placed on him are as dried up now as the sap in this crozier of yew wood. As the new High King well knows. Or should I say the old High King?

Mael Seachlainn You see this sceptre? Once it was mine. Then it was Brian's and now it is mine again. And it all proves nothing, nothing. The men of Leinster are still disaffected and in Munster and Connaught they're lying low but they hate me, and as for the Norsemen they're still selling Irish slave girls in Dublin.

Gormlai Brian is dead – that's one good thing. And it is a pity Sigurd is dead. But otherwise nothing has changed very much. Out there in Irish Ireland they're still tying rags on the briars by the holy wells and they still are scared of a lonely whitethorn. And I – who am lonely too – they still are scared of me. As for the foreigners, they are still here. And if ever they go, there are others will succeed them. No, no, no! Nothing was decided at Clontarf.
(*pause, then snatch of harp*)
Harper Does that suit you, poet?
Poet Anything you choose, harper.
(*longer stretch of harp, then break off*)
Harper Why are you not reciting? This is our farewell to Brian.
Poet I am tired of words. I spoke my farewell on the battlefield. You are lucky, harper.
Harper Why lucky?
Poet Words must be true or false; what you say on those strings is neither.
Harper I must do it alone then? The Farewell.

Persons from Porlock

The Story of a Painter

Was first broadcast in the BBC Third Programme on 30 August 1963 with the following cast:

HANK	*Jon Rollason*
SARAH	*Elizabeth Morgan*
PETER	*Peter Claughton*
MERVYN	*Norman Wynne*
MOTHER	*Mary O'Farrell*
MAGGIE	*Margaret Gordon*
DONALD	*Tom Watson*
BAILIFF	*Charles Leno*
DOCTOR	*Kenneth Hyde*
THE PERSON	*William Eedle*

It was Louis MacNeice's last production. When he went into the studio, after an expedition to the Yorkshire moors to record potholing effects, the illness which was to cause his death was already on him, and he died on 3 September.

When Coleridge failed to complete his dream poem, 'Kubla Khan', he said it was the fault of 'a person from Porlock' who had called to see him on business. To his 'no small surprise and mortification' this interruption destroyed his vision. Many lesser artists than Coleridge meet with interruptions of this sort. What follows is the story of an imaginary painter who had his Persons from Porlock.

Hank So there it is, Sarah. I've told hardly anyone else about this. I suppose it's made me rather anti-women. On the other hand it may be what made me take up painting.

Sarah What I don't understand, darling. . .

Hank Go on.

Sarah Is your mother dropping you cold like that?

Hank Well, my father insisted, you see.

Sarah No doubt. But seeing how small you were and how much you depended on her –

Hank I couldn't compete with this out-of-the-blue Don Juan. I forgot to tell you the first time he came he gave me a bar of marzipan. Marzipan! That was him.

Sarah Do you ever see your mother now, Hank?

Hank Of course not. I think she's in the South of France but I don't even know what her name is. It wasn't Don Juan she married, you see. Well, that's all; let's get back to the Guernica Exhibition.

Sarah Yes, wasn't it marvellous today!

Hank Funny to think Picasso was once a cubist.

Sarah Well, thank God all that lark's over. Being a woman I just never rose to this abstract thing. Now nobody need even try.

Hank How could they with what's going on in Europe! I sometimes feel guilty not being there, you know.

Sarah Europe?

Hank Spain, silly. And not to paint. To fight. Or do you think that also's to do with my mother?

Sarah Of course not, Hank.

Hank I never know my motives one hundred per cent – do you? Ready for bed, darling?

Sarah It's early. Let's go first to 'The Plough' and have a beer.

Hank Haven't got the price of one.

Sarah I have. Just. Us poor impoverished art students!

Hank I hope Peter's not in 'The Plough.'

Sarah Why?

Hank He enraged me today at the New Burlington. Saying Picasso would cash in on anything.

Sarah You shouldn't pay any attention, Peter's not really serious.

Hank Except about mountaineering. That's what he should be teaching.

Sarah Still, to be fair, we've got worse instructors than Peter.

Hank That's not saying much. Anyhow, I sometimes doubt if art can be taught at all. But, if Peter *is* in 'The Plough' and starts talking again about today's exhibition –

(fade up slight pub atmosphere and behind)

Peter You see, Hank, the point about today's exhibition is it's so jolly and flip. Have another pint?

Hank Yes, thank you.

Peter And you darling?

Sarah A half please.

Peter Two pints and a half please miss. Yes, people say it's all a practical joke. What's wrong with that? Practical's something that works.

Sarah But really, Peter! Furred cups and saucers and –

Peter Sex, my dear, sex. But the high spot was Dali in his diving suit. Trying to control those two borzois. You know what happened of course: the breathing apparatus went wrong. That will teach him to go diving in the New Burlington Galleries.

Hank When I think that only last year in those very same bloody galleries –

Sarah Yes. Picasso. Guernica.

Peter Guernica, my dear? Ancient history.

Hank People are still dying in Spain.

Peter And Picasso's still nobly declining to die. Anyhow, he painted Guernica just to cash in on the fashion.

Sarah Peter, how can you!

Hank Peter, if you're going to talk like that –

Peter Now don't get all starry-eyed and stupid. Only one good artist has been inspired by war and that's Goya.

Sarah I can't see how anyone comparing these two exhibitions –

Hank Surrealism! What does it add up to?

Peter What does Guernica add up to? Wait till we have a war of our own. Which we shall of course. Next year or the year after. And if you two think that's going to help your painting. . . It'll just cut you off from the Continent, you'll be more insular than ever.

Hank Are we any more insular than you?

Peter But of course you are, my dear boy. Partly because of your puri-
tanical mentalities but even more perhaps because you've never
painted abroad. Don't you realise that the light in this country –

Hank I don't think light is of primary importance.

Peter Oh, don't you.

Sarah Peter, what are *you* going to do when the war comes?

Peter Me? Camouflage perhaps. Hank will be too young for that.

Hank I don't think I'd want it anyway.

Peter You mean you'd rather fight?

Hank Whatever happens, I'll get through.

Sarah What do you mean, darling? Through it alive?

Hank No, through it as me. And that's not quite the word either.

Peter What an odd obscure fellow you are, Hank. You know, if you
two got married, they mightn't call Hank up so quickly.

Sarah That's impertinent of you, Peter.

Hank Yes, Peter, for God's sake! We've only just stopped being students
and we haven't any money between us – Anyhow, I'm too fond of
Sarah to marry her.

Sarah And that goes for me vice versa.

Peter Sorry, I seem to be obtuse. I'm taking a holiday next week.

Hank Snowdonia again?

Peter No, Yorkshire. And this time not up. Down.

Hank Meaning?

Peter Meaning speleology. Caves and pot-holes and things. In the
North they call it 'pot-oiling'.

Hank When I was little my mother used to read aloud to me. And one
book she read was by Jules Verne.

Peter *Journey to the Centre of the Earth*?

Hank That's right. It got me completely fascinated.

Peter Hank! You've been up mountains with me. Why don't you come
down a cave for a change?

Hank Well, in a way I'd like to but –

Sarah You go, darling. It will give me a chance to clean up the studio.

Hank Just a moment, both of you. There is one small snag.

Peter What is it?

Hank I suffer from claustrophobia.

   (*pause*)

Peter Oh. Well perhaps this might cure it. I knew a chap who had no

III

head for heights and he made a few parachute jumps and –

Hank It cured him?

Peter Completely.

Hank Right. I'll have a go.

Peter That's fine. I'll let Mervyn know.

Hank Mervyn?

Peter He used to be a Welsh Nationalist and this, I suspect, is a substitute. He has some rather quaint habits though. He's got to make jokes and they're always the same jokes. For example when he's leading, groping on ahead, and he calls back over his shoulder just to be sure you're O.K., well, how do you think he puts it?

(*cross fade pub atmosphere to cave atmosphere and behind*)

Mervyn (*calling*) How now, old mole?

(*silence*)

Hankey! I said: How now, old mole?

Hank (*calling*) Oh me? I'm O.K.

Mervyn (*calling*) How's the other old mole?

Hank (*calling*) Peter, you O.K.?

Peter (*calling*) I'm O.K. How are you?

Hank (*calling*) Fine.

(*to self*) I'm not though. Talk about back to the womb! Difference is the womb was soft.

Mervyn (*calling*) Hallo there! I've reached the pitch. Luncheon will be served immediately. One pork pie per head, bar of chocolate, tube of condensed milk.

Hank (*to self*) Moles. That tiny dead one on its back. Holding up its hands like a suppliant nun. Mummy took it away, threw it in the dustbin.

Mervyn Come on old mole.

Hank Here I am.

Mervyn Sit down. Don't impale yourself on a stalagmite.

Hank I don't see any stalagmites.

Mervyn There aren't any. Don't mind me, I'm just a mad hatter. But if you want stalactites and stalagmites, just wait till you see Skrimshank's.

Hank Skrimshank's?

Mervyn Hush, it's a secret. My Unknown Quantity. I've only so far explored the first chamber but, man, it's a symphony in dripstone. The chamber ends in a chimney, that's what we go down next.

Peter We?

Mervyn I'm talking about Skrimshank's.

Peter I guessed you were.

Hank Why is it called Skrimshank's?

Mervyn Skrimshank's Cave. I called it that. It was I who discovered it, you see. But I'm keeping it dark from the fraternity.

Peter Well, do I gather you're inviting both of us?

Mervyn To Skrimshank's? Yes, of course. We'll beat the bastard between us. Eat up your lunch boys, we've got to descend that pitch.

Peter Mervyn says Skrimshank's is a maze of galleries. With a number of chimneys and chambers and quite a few traps.

Mervyn That's all conjecture, mind you. How do you find this underworld, Hankey?

Hank Hank.

Mervyn Hank.

Hank I find it . . . excitingly timeless.

Mervyn That's right. You leave time outside. With the weather.

Peter The weather outside can affect us inside though.

Mervyn Yes, that's only too true. What else do you notice about it?

Hank Well, er. . .

Mervyn Don't you find it pure? Unsullied?

Hank Unsullied? Yes. I suppose so.

Mervyn I know so. And you like it?

Hank Oh yes.

Peter There, I knew your little trouble would be cured.

Mervyn Action stations! Out with the life-line, Peter. (*hums*) Have you seen the life-line man, the life-line man, the life-line man. . .
    (*fade out humming and cave atmosphere*)

Sarah The buses are hopeless, darling. Let's go by Underground.

Hank Damned if I will.

Sarah Why?

Hank It's under ground.

Sarah But seeing now you're a speleologist –

Hank Well that makes me feel sick too. But at least it has its compensations. Henry Moore for instance.

Sarah Henry Moore?

Hank He comes from Yorkshire too, you know. Remember those reclining figures with holes in them? That's the landscape all right. Well, if he can do it, why can't I? I'm set on getting through, I told you.

Sarah Through which, darling? Skrimshank's Cave or your problems as
an artist?

Hank Through both of course. But Skrimshank's will have to wait.
Mervyn's going off for two years to the Andes. Peter'll let me
know when he returns.

(*knock on door*)

Sarah Come in.

(*door opens*)

Sarah }
Hank } Oh, Peter!

Peter Heard the news?

Hank Mervyn's back?

Peter Russia have signed a pact with Germany.

Hank) What?
Sarah) No!

Peter So I'm going to rub up my camouflage.

Sarah You mean the war's on?

Peter The war's on, so Skrimshank's, I'm afraid, is off. Mervyn's on the
reserve, you know.

Hank I didn't know.

Peter What will you do, Hank?

Hank In the war? Wait till they conscript me.

Peter That's right. Don't volunteer.

Hank I won't. I've got things to paint.

Sarah I wonder where they'll send you.

Peter Maybe nowhere.

Hank Maybe. Or maybe worse than nowhere.

Mother Burma! But are things bad in Burma then?

Sarah They're cut off – surely you've heard that. So that must be why
I've not heard from him.

Mother So my poor lamb's in Burma! They told me you were the only
one who might know. You see, he hasn't any relatives. Present
company excepted and perhaps I don't really count.

(*pause*)

Or do I, my dear?

(*pause*)

Well, I can't force you to answer. Did he ever talk to you about me?

Sarah Yes.

Mother What did he say?

Sarah You can guess, can't you?

Mother Of course you would see it from his angle?

Sarah Mrs Hankey, why did you come back?

Mother Well, my dear, I just didn't want to be occupied. I mean Vichy France is not as bad as the other but even so, my dear, things were terribly difficult. And, when this awful war broke out, I was all set to go to Venezuela. Now I'll have to wait till it's over.

Sarah But first you'll wait to see your son?

Mother Yes, of course, my dear. What do you think I am?

Sarah May I ask you something?

Mother Anything you like, my dear.

Sarah It's not what I like but what I must. Why did you never get in touch with him before?

Mother Oh I tried to, my dear. Repeatedly. It was his father, you know.

Sarah His father's been dead some time.

Mother Yes, poor old man. Oh, I know I'm terribly to blame but I'm not quite as bad as you think. If you could only imagine how completely cut off I felt –

Sarah As completely as Hank?

Mother Year after year, but I can see it in your eyes: you just don't believe me, do you?

Sarah Mrs Hankey, would you like a drink?

Mother Oh, how very kind of you to ask me! But isn't it unfair with these war-time shortages –

Sarah Oh, *that's* not unfair. I can offer you beer or gin.

Mother I can't drink beer, I'm afraid, but if you could spare me a teeny weeny gin –

Sarah Say when. (*spot*)

Mother Just the width of an eyelash more, my dear. Thank you, you're a darling. What very good taste my boy has, taking up with a girl like you. By the way, talking of Venezuela, my friend out there is in oil –

('*all clear*')

What's that?

Sarah The All Clear.

Mother The All Cl—! Do you mean to say, while we've been talking, there's been an air raid on?

Sarah It's been on for hours – not that anything seems to have happened.

You must have missed the Alert.

Mother Good God! Well, cheers.

Sarah Would you like another?

Mother Well, in the circumstances –

Sarah You're welcome. But, while we've been talking, by the way, there's also been a world war on. It moved to France and you left there. It moved to Burma and he went there. Though whether there'll ever be an All Clear for that – he's cut off, can't you understand? Cut off in a pocket, surrounded by screaming Japs. For all you or I know, he's dead or a prisoner. And you sit there, dreaming of Venezuela.

Mother Now, I beg you, don't get hysterical; I know exactly how you feel, my dear. I feel all the same things too but I'm older and so I don't say them. All one can do is pray and have faith.

Sarah Pray and – Cheers!

Mother Cheers again, my dear.

(*fade up jungle night bird*)

Sergeant What was that, Mr Hankey?

Hank Some bloody night bird, Sergeant.

Sergeant Not a Jap imitating a bird?

Hank Could be a bird imitating a Jap. How far do you think they are now?

Sergeant Oh, fifty yards, as usual.

Hank Do you think they feel as blind as we do?

Sergeant Probably don't but they ought to. This is a blind bloody war. What you might call a ghost war. Always working in the dark and the mud and –

Hank How now, old mole? Sergeant, have you ever gone caving?

Sergeant How do you mean, Mr Hankey?

Hank Exploring caves – what they call speleology.

Sergeant Well, when I was a kid at the seaside –

Hank No, this is a serious thing like mountaineering. It's a perfectly grown-up thing. But those caves are darker than this even. There are also things called traps.

Sergeant What do they trap?

Hank The cavers.

Sergeant Just like us in the Fourteenth Army too. The whole bloody Arakan's a trap. We're all proper Charlies to be here.

(*pause: explosion of V2*)

Peter Good God, Sarah. Do you often have this sort of thing?

Sarah That's what we call a V2, Peter.

Peter Well, it shouldn't be allowed. Not the first time I'm home on leave from Shepheard's Hotel in Cairo.

Sarah Tell me, Peter, are you good at camouflage?

Peter Rather a dab in fact. Between ourselves I had a lot to do with Alamein. But to return to higher things –

Sarah No, Peter, I'm sorry, but definitely no.

Peter Hank wouldn't mind.

Sarah I'm not sure about that. But even if he wouldn't, I would.

Peter All right, let's drop it. This your latest?

Sarah It's my only painting in six months. I'm kept so busy in the Min. of Inf.

Peter 'm. It's interesting. A bit Little England, of course.

Sarah Well, what do you expect? As you said yourself, this war would enhance our insularity. But what, may I ask, have *you* been painting?

Peter I have painted one mural for a pasha. To amuse his women – which, I am told, it did.

Sarah Peter, will you go back to teaching after the war?

Peter I very much doubt it. I met some charming chaps in Shepheard's who think they can get me into advertising. That's the coming career, you know. Now if Hank was interested –

Sarah He wouldn't be. Hank will go straight on painting.

Peter He shouldn't.

Sarah Why the hell not?

Peter Because he uses painting as a therapy. Which is worse than people like me who use it for fun and games.

Sarah But supposing he does use painting as a therapy –

Peter He'll just be terribly disappointed. It won't be good painting and it won't be good therapy. Besides, Hank will always need money.

Sarah Yes, that I must admit: his tastes do get more and more extravagant.

Peter What about this cow of a mother of his? How's she off for the lolly?

Sarah Peter, seriously, I'm scared about that woman. And I don't even know if Hank will agree to see her.

Peter But he must, you must fix it, darling. And you'd better have all your plans ready. Any day now this war's going to come to an end.

Sarah The war in Europe, you mean. Hank's may go on for ever. I mean, the Japs won't surrender.

117

Peter Don't you worry: something will turn up to fix them.

Sarah I pray to God something does.

Peter To go back to Hank's mama, you're keeping in touch with her?

Sarah Oh, I've never seen her again and don't want to. Apart from anything else, she's on the bottle. But I promised to telephone as soon as Hank came home. It's some number in Shropshire.

Peter Safe hotel no doubt.

Sarah Oh, no doubt. But if Hank, as I suspect, won't ring her himself, why, then I'm prepared to do it for him.

    (pause: dialling and cross-fade to ringing of telephone)

Foreign Maid 'm? Yes? please. I am sorry. Madame is gone away it is now three weeks. Yes. Gone away. I am sorry. To Venezuela.

    (receiver replaced)

Sarah Hank! *(begins to sob)*

Hank It's what I expected. She's gone to Venezuela. But for God's sake stop crying. My mother means nothing to me now.

Sarah How do you know?

Hank Let her go to bloody Venezuela: you and I are going to the Victoria and Albert. To see what the boys have been up to. They, after all, are the civilisation I've been fighting for.

    (fade up picture gallery atmosphere and behind)

Voice A Makes one feel so terribly insular.

Voice B Not Matisse.

Voice A No, not Matisse, of course not.

Voice B But Picasso, yes.

Voice A Picasso, definitely yes. It's something we just can't do.

Voice B Perhaps it's because we weren't occupied.

    (up buzz of voices and behind)

Voice C Jennifer, have you seen that? What do you think it is?

Voice D It could be a woman, mum.

Voice C A woman? With one eye sideways and one eye frontways –

Voice D It's what they call distortion, mum.

Voice C I'll say it's what they call distortion! I've a good mind to ask for our money back.

    (up buzz and behind again)

Peter Hank!

Hank Peter!

Peter Well, you old so-and-so! You're looking terribly well, Burma must be healthy.

Hank You should try it some day.

Peter So you've just got back in time for your idol's exhibition.

Hank My idol?

Peter Picasso. Well, I wouldn't mean Matisse, would I?

Hank He *was* my idol; it's funny.

Peter What's funny?

Hank Well, I don't think he is any more, it may be I'm just out of touch but ... you know how I felt at the time of the Guernica exhibition?

Peter Well, you've got older since then.

Hank I've been in battle since then. And now – oh, perhaps I've gone blind but I don't think Picasso's saying anything. It's all too bloody virtuoso.

Peter Well, I'm more than inclined to agree with you. What about your own work, Hank?

Hank Well, you don't think I painted in the jungle, do you? I've lost five years and now I've lost the studio. But the moment I can find four walls and a roof –

Sarah I know of a studio, darling. A huge one, just the place for us. We could cook there, sleep there, everything. The only trouble is it's shockingly expensive.

Hank Oh, don't worry about that, I've got my army gratuity. Just tell me where it is and we'll take it.

Peter That's the spirit; more power to your elbows. But Hank, if you do need money, just let me know because I've got a proposition –

Hank Thank you, Peter, at the moment I just don't fancy propositions. All I need is a canvas and a brush. And four walls and a roof and Sarah. And then I can get through. I know I can.

(*fade out art gallery background*)

No, I can't! I can't! I can't! I can't!

Sarah If you're going to destroy that canvas too, I'd like you at least to pay me for it.

Hank Don't sound so acid, Sarah.

Sarah Sorry, darling, I saw your point with the last one but this one was coming on well.

Hank Here you are: paint over it. Sarah, I'm sorry; I've had it.

Sarah Had what?

Hank The painting business. I lost most of it in Burma and the little bit left over I lost in Venezuela. And now go on: despise me for my self-pity.

Sarah Hank, come and sit here beside me; I've got things to say to you. I know I've said them before but –

Hank It's no good saying them again, I take that back about Venezuela. But as far as Burma is concerned –

Sarah Darling, I know it was ghastly.

Hank It wasn't, you know, all of it. Some of it was bloody funny and some of it was even inspiring. There was one particular morning when the word inspiration applied. This was after the monsoon, there was sun, one could really see things. There was a river with bamboos reflected in it. I thought to myself: here it comes, this is vision again, I've still got it. And then the thing happened – the worst thing I met in Burma.

　　(*pause*)

Sarah Go on, darling.

Hank The worst thing I met was the worst thing I did. I was looking idly – yes, idly – through my binoculars and there at two hundred yards, bang in the open, was a tiny Jap soldier enjoying a crap. Just having a crap on his own without a care in the world. Well, Lance-Corporal Potter by ill luck was standing beside me with a rifle and it suddenly, just for the hell of it, occurred to me to try my eye. I never really expected to hit him – as you know, I'm not a good shot – and when I did I almost shook hands with myself. Lance-Corporal Potter was properly impressed too. I was so pleased I felt it had made my day. But that only lasted half a minute or so. And then I thought, well I thought what a thing to do. And I suddenly hated not only the war but myself. And as for the vision that had just been with me, that finished it.

Sarah I understand, darling, but that must have happened to so many people. It's all part of it, surely?

Hank All part of what? Of a lost lousy world. Look at what ended that whole war. We were delighted at the time of course. By the way, you remember that letter I got this morning?

Sarah About artists' careers being interrupted by the war?

Hank Interrupted! The understatement of 1946. Have we got a Coleridge in the house?

Sarah Coleridge? I'll look.

Hank When one's interrupted one can't pick it up again. It's happened to me all my life. My mother's lover with the bar of marzipan, and then the war itself –

Sarah Here you are; service! Collected Poems of Coleridge.

Hank Now wait till I find it; this is all about me, darling. Here you are: 'Kubla Khan: or, A Vision in a Dream'. Bamboos reflected in the river and blue mountains beyond. A vision in Burma on a sunny morning. This is what old Coleridge said:

(reading) 'On awaking he appeared to himself to have a distinct recollection of the whole, and taking his pen, ink, and paper, instantly and eagerly wrote down the lines that are here preserved. At this moment' – here it comes, Sarah – 'At this moment he was unfortunately called out by a person on business from Porlock, and detained by him above an hour, and on his return to his room, found, to his no small surprise and mortification, that though he still retained some vague and dim recollection of the general purport of the vision, yet, with the exception of some eight or ten lines and images,' – look at that thing on the easel there – 'all the rest had passed away like the images on the surface of a stream into which a stone had been cast, but, alas! without the after restoration of the latter.' There you are, Sarah, that's me. No small surprise and mortification. It's happened before and it will happen again.

(telephone rings: receiver lifted)

Sarah   Yes? . . . Oh, Peter? . . .

It's Peter for you, he's got one of his famous propositions. But watch it, darling. Don't commit yourself.

Hank   Hullo, Peter! . . . What? . . . Next week-end? Yes, I'm doing nothing. I'm always doing nothing these days. . . No, she won't mind. Yes, I'd love to.

(receiver replaced)

(fade up cave atmosphere and behind)

Mervyn   (calling) How now, old mole?

Hank   I'm all right, Mervyn.

Mervyn   Not dropping those pitons are you?

Hank   I'm not dropping anything, Mervyn.

Mervyn   Only the gentle dew from your armpits. Well, join me here and we'll wait for Peter.

(scrabbling of rope-soled shoes on rock)

You see. I told you about the dripstone. Stalactites and stalagmites, gypsum flowers, the lot!

Hank   What I like about caves is their names.

Mervyn   Oh yes, their names, man, they're marvellous. Alum Pot and Gaping Ghyll, Lost John's Cave and Wookey Hole.

Peter   Here I am, Columbus. And here's the missing life-line. So we're all set for the drop. How deep is that damned chimney?

121

Mervyn I'm in no hurry; sit down and get your breath, man. Hank here
    and I were just talking about caves.

Peter How did you stumble on that subject?

Mervyn What a pity it is, you know, once the trippers are in. Take the
    biggest cave in the world, the Calsbad Cavern in New Mexico.
    Do you know it has an intake of five hundred persons per hour?
    They whiz down by elevator eight hundred feet and what do they
    find when they get there? A quick feed restaurant and a male voice
    choir on record. Commercialisation! You'd think we had enough
    on the surface.

Peter (*low*) Talking of commercialisation, Hank, you won't forget –

Hank No, I won't.

Peter It shouldn't interfere with your own work, you can always do that
    on the side.

Hank On the side? Oh, yes. Of course.

Peter So that's a date? We'll lunch with Alec next week?

Hank And take a long spoon. Yes, that's a date.

Mervyn Action stations, boys! Shoulder your tackle! Chimney's just
    thirty yards ahead. Onward Christian cavers!

Peter How deep is it, Mervyn?

Mervyn How would I know? Fifty feet, perhaps sixty. We'll drop a stone
    and find out, but I hope your life-line's not rotten.
    (*hums*) Have you seen the life-line man, the life-line man, the life-
    line man,
    Have you seen the life-line man
    (*fading*) Who lives in Skrimshank's Cave?
      (*lose cave atmosphere: pause: door opens*)

Hank (*singing on approach*):
    Have you seen the life-line man, the life-line man, the life-line man,
    Have you seen the life-line man
    Who lives in W.1?

Sarah Hank! You've obviously had a good lunch.
    Where's Peter?

Hank Left him with Alec.

Sarah Alec?

Hank The chap he wanted me to meet.

Sarah So you're on Christian names already?

Hank It's a Christian name world, Alec's.

Sarah And you're proposing to join it?

Hank We need the money, Sarah.

Sarah   And how will you get it?

Hank   By drawing things.

Sarah   Advertisements you mean?

Hank   Oh, no. Illustrations to women's magazines. And strip cartoons if
I'm lucky. Oh, maybe an ad just once in a while. I've appointed
Alec my agent.

Sarah   Mervyn rang up when you were out.

Hank   Mervyn! Why?

Sarah   To send you his apologies. The next expedition's off. He's suddenly been invited to some do in the Pyrenees. Some archaeo-
logical do. But about Skrimshank's: he says when he comes back
to tell you: all you need now is more rope.

Hank   All I need now is more rope?

Sarah   You remember the proverb, of course?

Hank   Sarah, you're a bitch.

Sarah   I'm a what?

Hank   A bitch. B-I-T-C-H. I thought you'd be pleased that we're now in
the money.

Sarah   That *we're* now in the money?

Hank   Well, you don't suppose that, when I'm rich, I'm going to leave
you out of it!

   (*pause: fade up ringing phone: receiver lifted*)

Maggie   Hullo! . . . Yes, of course this is Maggie . . . Oh, Sarah darling!
After all this time! Whatever have you been doing with yourself?
. . . Yes, I *am* still looking for someone to share the flat. . . You
mean *you* would like to? But what about Hank? . . . Out! How do
you mean out? . . . But lots of people are commercial artists. . .
Yes, I've seen those strips they're very clever. I don't think one
should be snob about it. . . On the bottle too? But that's nothing
new, darling. . . Worse? How much worse? . . . Oh really? Well,
you know you're always welcome *here*. . . Oh, as soon as that?
Marvellous, darling, I'll expect you.

   (*receiver replaced: pause: fade up Peter*)

Peter   Well, that's my second point. And my third point, Hank – you're
not listening!

Hank   I got your first point, Peter: that's all I need. You got me into all
this and now you're running me out of it.

Peter   I'm doing no such thing, I'm merely tipping you off. Alec says
they're getting tired of it. You're always being so behind-hand.

Hank   Well, when I'm beforehand, what happens? The Art Editor sends it back to me. Look at this: they even rejected this. Because I drew the bride's nose straight: they said it should have been tiptilted. As if brides couldn't wear straight noses! Women's magazines! You can have them.

Peter   But it's not just the women's magazines. Alec says your comics for teenagers –

Hank   You're out of date. I've packed that in already.

Peter   Well, now we come to the worst thing. Worst because it's the most lucrative. That daily strip cartoon of yours in the Daily –

Hank   Stop! I know it brings in the money but I just can't keep up the pace. If I work till four in the morning I can only do two in the day. I'm going to pack that in too.

Peter   But you told me it had been an education.

Hank   That was two years ago.

Peter   But you'll keep on the women's mags?

Hank   Yes, if they'll keep me on.

Peter   Well, that brings me to – forgive me mentioning this but Alec – well, frankly, it's about your drinking. Alec says unless –

Hank   Alec says! Alec says! Sarah sent that one up long ago.

Peter   I wish you'd listen.

Hank   Do you know how long it is since she left?

Peter   Sarah? Three years? Four? How long?

Hank   I can't remember! But she never came back for her paintings. Those are all hers in the corner.

Peter   And that canvas on the easel?

Hank   That's mine. That surprised you, Peter, didn't it?
> (pause)

Well, come on, what do you think of it?
> (pause)

Peter   'm. It looks as if you've joined the British Romantics. No, that's not a sneer. The British Romantics with a difference.

Hank   Can you guess what that was suggested by?

Peter   Skrimshank's?

Hank   Got it in one. Perhaps you could have taught art if you'd gone on.

Peter   You think it's a pity?

Hank   Maybe. It's a far greater pity that Mervyn's living abroad.

Peter   But haven't you heard? He's back.

Hank   Back! Since when?

Peter   Two months ago, actually. And any day now he's going to have another crack at Skrimshank's.

124

Hank *I've* not heard anything about it.

Peter Well, er . . . You mean you'd still be interested?

Hank I'll always be interested. Tell Mervyn, will you, I'm interested.

Peter Yes, of course, when I see him. There's nothing definite yet you know.

Hank And tell Alec I'm through.

Peter What?

Hank Tell Alec I'm through with commercials.

Peter Why should I?

Hank That's right. Why should you? He's not your agent, he's mine. You can't sack him but I can. And I *will*; it will be a pleasure.

Peter Hank, you mustn't! You'll ruin your career.

Hank Ruin my what? I'm about to cross the Rubicon. That's the Rubicon there. That little black object with a dial on it. That's my Rubicon, Peter.

Peter Now, Hank –

Hank And I cross it simply by dialling.

    (*dialling and fade out*)

Maggie I saw Peter today, Sarah.

Sarah Yes, Maggie?

Maggie He told me something that should please you.

Sarah What's that?

Maggie Hank has dropped the commercials and is starting to paint again.

    (*pause*)

    Well, aren't you interested?

Sarah Not particularly.

Maggie Well, of all the strange girls –

Sarah Three years ago I would have been.

Maggie Peter's furious, of course. It's made trouble between him and this Alec man.

Sarah Is Hank still hitting it hard?

Maggie Oh, I don't know anything about that. Though Peter did say he was high when he made the great renunciation.

Sarah Dutch courage. No. It won't work.

Maggie Darling, why don't you go and see him? After taking a step like that he must need someone to talk to.

Sarah Hank can find plenty of sounding-boards.

    (*fade up moderate clapping*)

Hank Thank you, ladies and gentlemen. I very much appreciate the

quite undeserved speech of thanks that the gentleman in the Old
Etonian tie –

1st Voice It's not as a matter of fact.

(*laughter*)

Hank Old Carthusian tie made in response to my lecture. I've enjoyed
coming here more than I expected. And I hope I've said one or
two things that may give you to think.

(*giggles and whispering*)

About Henry Moore, for instance. Did I make my point about
Henry Moore?

2nd Voice You did. Several times.

(*giggles*)

Hank The point is this, you see; the point is this. The point is – oh yes:
in this country for the first time since, for the first time, in this
country sculpture has now got ahead of painting. So we painters
have got to catch up, we've got to beat the bloody hour-glass.

3rd Voice Language!

(*laughter*)

Hank What are you laughing about? Yes, that's right, beat the bloody
hour-glass. Action stations and get on with it. But when I say
action stations I don't mean action painting. I'll tell you a secret: I
don't like action painting. When I want to paint I paint and, when
I want action, know what I do? I go down a bloody pot-hole.

3rd Voice Language!

(*laughter*)

Hank Who said language? I'll tell you something. You people don't
speak *my* language. But let me tell you something. Next week I'm
going exploring. Exploring a cave nobody knows about. And the
man I'll be with, the man who discovered that cave – he's worth
all you lot put together –

4th Voice Shame!

Hank He speaks my language all right. Because I'm an artist and he's a
speleologist. Yes, old Mervyn speaks my language.

(*fade up cave background, with stream, and behind*)

Mervyn (*calling*) How now, old mole?

Donald (*calling*) Wait for me, Mervyn, my light's gone.

Mervyn (*calling*) Hasn't Peter got a light?

Donald (*calling*) Yes, of course.

Mervyn (*calling*) You wait for him then. I'm busy.

(*pause*)

126

Donald (*calling*) Hurry up, Peter, my light's gone.

Peter (*calling*) Coming, Donald.

    (*effect of rope-soles on rock*)

    (*to self*) Really, this boy Donald! First he drops the eats in the stream . . . next he gets stuck in a squeeze . . . and now for good measure his light's gone. Still we had to have three.

    Hullo, Donald! Got your spare battery?

Donald I've got no spare battery.

Peter Then I'll give you mine. Hold this torch.

Donald Peter, I'm loving every minute of this.

Peter Are you?

Donald Greatest fun I ever had in my life. I shouldn't say it, I suppose, but I'm glad your friend had 'flu.

Peter Between ourselves, he hadn't.

Donald Eh?

Peter Mervyn wouldn't take him.

Donald But why? I thought he was quite an old hand at it.

Peter He's become, well, perhaps a rather shaky hand. And he didn't really like it all that much. He suffers from claustrophobia, you see.

Hank (*shouting*) Let me out! Let me out, let me out, let me out!

Maggie But you are out, Hank, you're in the park, you've just been having a nap on the grass.

Hank The park! Who am I with?

Maggie Me! But you mustn't shout. People are staring at you, ducky.

Hank Me? Who's me? Who's you?

Maggie Maggie. Don't you remember? I called on you this afternoon and then you took me out to dinner.

Hank What did we have for dinner?

Maggie Oh really, Hank! Those perfectly lovely scampi and –

Hank He wouldn't take me down his bloody cave.

Maggie What cave? Who wouldn't?

Hank You wouldn't know! Who are you, anyway?

Maggie I told you. I'm a friend of Sarah's.

Hank Oh Sarah. How is Sarah?

Maggie I told you: she's quite all right.

Hank Did Sarah ask you to call on me?

Maggie Well, not exactly but –

Hank Kiss me.

Maggie No, no, Hank, not in the park.

127

Hank Yes, that's right, we must wait till Sarah goes.

Maggie Sarah's not here.

Hank I thought you just said she was.

Maggie Darling, you're a little confused. I'm going to take you home now.

Hank Yes, take me home. And then you know what? You and me'll have a little nightcap.

Maggie A little one, yes; not a big one.

Hank Why not a big one?

Maggie Because tomorrow you've got to see Tony.

Hank Who's Tony?

Maggie Oh God, darling, I told you! The man who can get you in on television.

Hank Oh yes, I remember. Animated cartoons. Damned if I want to do those.

Maggie Now don't be naughty. You promised. Come along, get up. Easy now, I'm taking you home and giving you a tiny nightcap and then I'm setting your alarm clock.

Hank No, no clock. No time under ground, you know.

Maggie I'll set it for 11.30. That will get you to lunch on time.

Hank Don't want lunch.

Maggie It's with Tony.

Hank Tony? Oh yes.

Maggie You promised.

Hank Then you stay with me till the alarm goes off.

Maggie I'm afraid I can't do that.

Hank Oh yes, Sarah, you can. You always used to, damn it.

Maggie Hank! I am not Sarah.

Hank Then there's no obstacle. First taxi home, then tiny nightcap, then set alarm clock, then bed for both.

Maggie Not for both. For you.

Hank But I can't sleep alone, Sarah. The dark's full of traps, stream keeps rising, poor old moles get drowned. Little drowned nuns with little hands still praying.

Maggie We're going now.

Hank That's right: going. Going to nightcap, then bed, then alarm clock. Alarm and despondency, alarms and excursions. . .

　　(*alarm clock*)

Sarah! Turn that off!

　　(*alarm clock out*)

My God, who are *you*? Have we committed adultery?

Maggie That didn't arise, darling.

Hank Then let it arise now.

    (*pause: fade up restaurant background and behind*)

Tony So you see, Hank – sorry you've eaten nothing – when we saw those strip cartoons it struck us all simultaneously that your style was just like Bill's.

Hank Bill's?

Tony I've been telling you: Bill Trueman. The man I want you to work for.

Hank I don't believe my style is just like his. What would I have to do?

Tony Just what I explained. He does the key drawings, you do the fill-ins.

Hank Why can't I do the key drawings.

Tony Because animation is a very special technique. If you have a real flair for it – and my guess is you probably have – why, then, within a year or six months or even sooner you can branch out on your own and form your own animation company. Just as Bill Trueman did himself. How does that prospect tempt you? Orders coming in from here, there, and everywhere. The tobacco people, the ice-cream people, the detergent people, the lot! That's where you may be in a year or so.

    (*fade out restaurant atmosphere*)

Maggie Darling! A man rang up today. He wants you to animate whatsits-name toffee.

Hank Oh hell, Maggie! I've enough on my plate already. If I take on one more contract, I *will* have to get another assistant.

    (*fade up piano – one finger – tune of 'have you seen the mocking bird?'*)

Peter Sarah, look at the screen! This commercial.

Sarah Ugh! What about it?

Peter It's Hank's.

Sarah That beastly little bear with toothache?

Peter Not toothache, darling, that's toffee.

    (*recorded voice of singer:*)

Have you seen the Toffee Bear, the Toffee Bear, the Toffee Bear,

Have you seen the Toffee Bear?

Yum! Yum! Yum! Yum! Yum!

    (*recording out*)

Sarah Poor Hank! How ghastly for him!

Peter Sarah?

Sarah Yes?

Peter If I may ask, why do you go on living here?

Sarah Why, you know: I took over the lease two years ago.

Peter Yes, from Maggie: that's what I mean.

Sarah But I'm the sole tenant now.

Peter Well *that*, in fact, is what I mean. I'd have thought the associations – After all, we all know where Maggie's living.

Sarah Peter, you're bloody impertinent.

(*pause: fade up Hank whistling toffee bear tune*)

Jock Mr Hankey!

Hank (*stopping whistling*) What, Jock?

Jock I've got a complaint to make.

Hank Well I've a complaint to make too. You are still unable to get the rhythm. I've just been flipping over the cells and I'm afraid it won't do. Sorry, Jock, but it's bad animation.

Jock Yes, I agree, it won't do. You're three weeks behind with my wages. Norman and I are fed up.

Hank I've explained to Norman and you: I'm in the same position. No one ever pays me on the dot –

Jock That's your affair, you're the boss. But speaking as a wage slave, wages are wages. And how with all your contracts you can get so behind hand. . .

Maggie Why with all your contracts you're always in debt is something beyond my understanding.

Hank Like many other things.

Maggie A month or two ago you had four figures in the bank; now you're in the red. I just can't think how you manage it.

Hank Can't you? Take a good look round this studio – or rather it used to be a studio, now it's like a call-girl's dream.

Maggie Thank you.

Hank You might also look in that pier glass. What you have on your exquisite torso isn't exactly sackcloth.

Maggie Well, at least your drink bills are down.

Hank I told you to stop that parrot cry. 'I saved him from a drunkard's grave. I saved him for the commercials.' Twenty-five frames per second which means about sixteen drawings, most of which I have to do myself because my assistants are imbeciles – Maggie, I think I've had it!

Maggie Had what?

130

Hank Commercials.

Maggie Oh, and what are you going to do then?

Hank What I was born to do. Paint.

Maggie Hadn't you better wait till you're out of the red?

Hank No, Maggie: life's too short.

Maggie You've not even paid the rent and the rates.

Hank I'm forty-two and I've never had a show. It's time I did.

Maggie But you haven't any pictures.

Hank That can be corrected. It will take me two years.

Maggie What am *I* to do for the next two years then?

Hank Whatever you like. Stay on here if you like.

Maggie That's very kind of you.

Hank But I warn you: I'll have to clear the decks. Once I start to paint I can't have all these carpets and armchairs and things. And I'll need all the cupboards available. That one and that one and that one –

Maggie That one's my wardrobe.

Hank Not any more it's not.

Maggie Hank!

Hank What do you mean 'Hank'?

Maggie So you're now even grudging me a wardrobe!

Hank You can hang your clothes in the bathroom.

Maggie I can what?

Hank It was you who wanted a bathroom – it cost me – what? – to put it in.

Maggie I didn't know you'd paid for it yet.

Hank I haven't but that's not the point. You wanted that bathroom. Now you can hang your clothes in it.

Maggie I'm not removing a single thing from my wardrobe.

Hank If you're not, I am.

Maggie Hank!

> (*double doors of cupboard thrown violently open – hangers pushed along rail*)

Hank Here! Catch!

> (*dress on hanger clatters on floor*)

And this (*effect*). And this! (*effect*). . . And this and this and this and (*effect*). And this disgusting monstrosity.

Maggie Hank! Stop it!

> (*effect*)

And this little piece that's ten years too young for you.

Maggie O.K. Where are my suitcases?

> (*long pause: fade up Hank whistling 'Onward Christian Soldiers'*)

Peter Hank, I'm astonished.

Hank (*stopping whistling*) What by, Peter?

Peter By all this work. You've done all these in a year, you say?

Hank One year and one month.

Peter Including those jumbo-sized canvases? Hate to think what they cost.

Hank Never mind the quantity. What about the quality?
  (*pause*)

Peter May I be candid?

Hank Of course.

Peter I don't think people will like them.

Hank Look, I don't want to know if they'll be in the top ten. I'm asking if they're good.

Peter To tell you the truth, Hank, I don't really know. You see you used to be a man for line but the line seems to have gone.

Hank I had too much of that in the cartoons. But you're wrong: it's still there – underneath.

Peter Trouble is painting's a visual medium.

Hank If you look long enough, the line will emerge.

Peter At art shows people don't look very long. You want to sell your pictures, don't you?

Hank Of course. I've got debts to pay off.

Peter What are you going to ask for these?

Hank Nothing less than three figures.

Peter Even the tiddly ones?

Hank Even the tiddly ones.

Peter It's your first show, remember.

Hank 'How can I forget?' says balding young artist. If the war hadn't happened, if Alec hadn't happened, if Maggie hadn't happened – Do you ever see Sarah now?

Peter Once or twice a week.

Hank I'd like to have her opinion.

Peter Well, ask her to come and look at them.

Hank How can I! I've only seen her once since the Maggie business.

Peter She doesn't seem to resent that, you know.

Hank No?

Peter Oh, she resents Maggie all right but, as between herself and you, she'd admit it was she who left you. She's a very honest girl, you know, Hank.

Hank Of course I know. That's why I want her to see these pictures.

She's the one person I could trust to give me an honest opinion.

Sarah If I'm to give you my honest opinion, I think what you mean is valid – it's something that comes from the depths – but I don't think you're getting it over. There are four to five where you do – take this one for instance –

Hank I like that one myself. Do you know what it is?

Sarah A dead mole.

Hank My God, you're perceptive, Sarah. Most people would think it was an abstract.

Sarah It's a dead mole and it's praying. Of course, I must confess, you told me that story.

Hank What others do you like?

Sarah Well, that – and that – and that.

Hank And this?

Sarah No, definitely not.

Hank What's wrong with it?

Sarah Nearly everything.
        (*pause*)

Hank I know what's wrong with my work. You used to be here to criticise.

Sarah But you didn't get through even then.

Hank I think I might now. Will you come back, darling?

Sarah You are funny!

Hank Funny?

Sarah Egocentric. This is not a bad one either. I like the beam of light playing on that fan-vaulting, bringing out those blues and greens and yellows –

Hank You think it's a church, do you?

Sarah Isn't it?

Hank No, it's a cave. The first chamber in Skrimshank's.

Sarah Oh dear, old Skrimshank's! I'd forgotten Skrimshank's.

Hank Forgotten? I wish I could! Mervyn refused to take me the last time.

Sarah Why?

Hank Why do you think? And Peter tells me they all get stuck at a trap and Mervyn's named it the Stygian Trap – sometimes his humour is a trifle macabre.

Sarah I've forgotten. A trap means. . .?

Hank It's where there's an underground stream and the rock comes down so low that you can't get through without swimming under water. Mervyn's been abroad ever since then, so nobody's conquered that trap yet. But I hope to be in on it yet. What do you think of this?

Sarah Hank! Can't you really tell the difference? Between these two.

Hank No, I can't. They're all equally me.

     (pause)

Sarah In that case I'd better come back. I'm a fool of course but –

Hank Sarah!

Sarah And we'll have to work like mad if you're going to have your show next spring.

     (fade up art gallery background and behind)

Voice A Can't make head or tail of it.

Voice B Did you ever hear of this man Hankey before?

Voice A What's the point of painting in black on black?

Voice X How he's got the nerve to ask three hundred for that!

Voice Y Rather a come-down after that German group.

Voice X I notice nothing's been sold so far.

     (fade out background)

Director of Gallery Well, Mr Hankey, I know it's disappointing. But I warned you: these things are a gamble. It's a pity you clashed with the Young German Exhibition – and then there's that disciple of Pollock's –

Hank Yes, emperors all of them.

Director Emperors?

Hank Emperors' new clothes. Not a bit like my stuff.

Director Well, at least we did sell five. Though not, I agree, at the prices in the catalogue. And I think, if I may say so, you were rash to spend so much on the frames. At a guess these must have averaged ten pounds . . . twelve?

Hank More like fifteen. And I haven't paid for them all yet.

Director Fifteen? And what about the –

     (fade up knocking on door: door opens)

Bailiff Are you Mr Hankey? I expect you can guess who I am. I have to present you with this.

Hank What is it?

Bailiff Well, sir, I'm afraid it's a Court Order. And it's my duty to quarter myself upon you until such time as this debt is paid. But I'll try not to get in your way, sir; it's fortunate perhaps you have such commodious premises.

134

(*pause*)

Hank Supposing I write you a cheque?

Sarah Hank, you know you can't!

Bailiff I'm sorry, sir; I couldn't accept a cheque. I am only allowed to take payment in cash.

Sarah Show me that bit of paper. Good God! Never mind, I'll be back with the cash in an hour or two. Give the gentleman a cup of tea.

Hank But, Sarah, wherever are you going?

Sarah Never mind, darling.

(*door opens and closes: pause*)

Hank Do you really want tea? Or would you prefer Scotch?

Bailiff Oh no, sir, thank you. Tea is my customary tipple.

Hank You don't mind if I have Scotch?

Bailiff Naturally not, sir. De gustibus, as they say. . . Excuse my asking, sir, but are you a professional artist?

Hank What do you think all these things are?

Bailiff I can see they are paintings, sir, but I thought it might just be your hobby.

Hank Hobby! It's my bloody cross.

Bailiff Oh. There's something else I'd like to ask, sir.

Hank Ask away.

Bailiff This is purely professional curiosity, as the question, it transpires, will not arise, but this very large room we're in, is this your only sitting-room?

Hank This room is a studio but it's also my only sitting-room, *and* my only bedroom.

Bailiff Hm, in that case there wouldn't be much to distrain on. Please forgive me, sir, I'm talking to myself. We'd have to leave you the bed of course. And most of the rest would appear to be the tools of your trade.

Hank 'Appear to be' is right.

Bailiff If I may importune you again, sir, why do you have more than one easel?

Hank Because I need more than one.

Bailiff That one there, sir, surely is an exceptionally large easel.

Hank It is. It cost me a hundred.

Bailiff Excuse me, sir. A hundred?

Hank Once upon a time it belonged to a very famous artist.

Bailiff I see. Raises an interesting problem. The question of course will not arise but –

135

(kettle whistles off)

Hank Sorry. That's the kettle.

Bailiff (to self) Interesting problem, yes... Was your easel really necessary?... A hundred? Remarkable.

Hank (approach) How do you like your tea? Strong? Weak? Medium?

Bailiff Just as it comes, sir, just as it comes. I notice you possess an exceptionally large tea-pot.

    (pouring effect)

Hank Well, see if you can drink your way through it before the lady comes back. And I'll drink my way through this.

Bailiff Not through all the bottle, I trust, sir!

Hank That depends when she comes back.

    (bottle and glass business)

    Well, cheers.

Bailiff Cheers, sir.

    I've often wondered how it feels to be an artist.

Hank How does it feel to be a bailiff?

Bailiff It is rather... an ambivalent feeling. On the whole, sir, I am quite relieved that my little boy's not going to follow in my footsteps. He is only eight and a half but he knows what he's going to be already.

Hank And what is he going to be?

Bailiff A racing driver, sir.

Hank Good for him. Well, cheers.

Bailiff Oh didn't I say cheers? Cheers, sir.

    (fade and pause)

Sarah Hank! How could you! This bottle's empty.

Hank He distrained on it. He drank it. Didn't you?

Sarah Didn't who?

Hank My friend over there.

Sarah Your friend over there's just left. With his pockets full of fivers. He asked to be remembered to you.

Hank He distrained on your gin as well.

Sarah You mean that on top of all that Scotch you –

Hank No, he did; didn't you, sir?

Sarah Hank, there's no one there.

Hank Yes there is, there always is. 'Who is the third who walks always beside me?' Tell you what, let's all three go out and celebrate.

Sarah Hank, you'd better go to bed.

136

Hank No, we must go out and celebrate. I've got the car round the back and –

Sarah You've got the car round the back?

Hank If you don't believe me, look from the bathroom window.
(*humming*) Onward Christian painters
  Marchin' through the muck –

Sarah (*approach*) Hank! Give me the keys.

Hank What keys?

Sarah The car keys.

Hank Haven't got them.

Sarah Oh blast you! (*pause*) What's this in your pocket then?

Hank This is the key of the Kingdom.

Sarah Hank! Listen! Go to bed. I'll be back when I've put it in the garage. But do be good and go to bed: you're nine-tenths out already.

Hank Right. I'll be good. I'll go to bed. See you later, darling. See you later, sir.

Sarah (*moving off*) Ach!
  (*door bangs: pause: telephone rings for some time: receiver lifted*)

Hank Yes? Who is it? . . . Who?! . . . Hospital? What hospital? . . . Who? . . . In my car? Yes? . . . How bad is she? . . . Broken ribs and – I'll come round at once – . . . Oh I see, tomorrow. Tomorrow then. Give her my love. Tell her I'll see her tomorrow.
  (*receiver replaced: pause*)

Sarah The flowers are lovely, darling. How's your hangover?

Hank The worst ever.

Sarah I wish it was the last ever.

Hank I'm sorry, Sarah.

Sarah The ironic thing is it's I who'll be losing my licence.

Hank Oh they'll probably just endorse it.

Sarah I'm afraid not, Hank – driving across the red like that. I'm lucky not to have killed anyone.

Hank But you never drive across the red.

Sarah I was thinking about you, darling.
  (*pause*)

Hank Darling, what was the name of that doctor?

Sarah What doctor?

Hank The one you once asked me to go to. You know: the one who does the Cure.

Sarah Oh, Doctor Butler. Why?

Hank This time I'll go to him. He can slang me all he wants but –

Sarah He won't slang you, darling. But you'll have to tell him all about yourself.

Doctor And that, of course, has a great deal to do with it. The last twist of the knife was when your mother went to Venezuela. All along, subconsciously, you felt it was your fault. It's appalling to think how many mothers have made their sons alcoholics. For, not to mince words, Mr Hankey, that's what you are. Your mother started it, your failure in the art world continued it. As an artist you've always felt inadequate: therefore, subconsciously, you set out to destroy yourself. It's just because you're a creative person and because in the creative field –

Hank Doctor Butler, I wish you'd stop using that word.

Doctor I can't. For you it's the key word.

    (*pause*)

Hank What are you going to do to me?

Doctor Nothing very frightening. First we'll give you some injections to clear your system of alcohol. Next come some dashes of vitamins. After that it's up to you. We'll supply you with pills but you'll have to promise to take them.

Hank I've heard of those pills. They're the ones that make you feel like death.

Doctor Only if you drink – and then you'd feel worse than death. But you will take them, won't you?

Hank Yes, I will, Doctor; thank you.

Doctor Good man. And, I assure you, in no time at all you'll feel different. You'll find yourself able to work again, you'll even be fit to take up your caving again, or pot-holing or whatever you call it, if you still want to keep up that hobby.

Hank Oh, it's more than a hobby, Dr Butler. But I don't know if Mervyn will take me again.

    (*fade up cave*)

Mervyn (*ordinary voice*) How now, old moles?

Donald Fine, Mervyn, fine.

Mervyn And you, Hank?

Hank Yes.

Mervyn You both had a long enough rest?

Donald Yes.

Hank Yes, Mervyn.

Mervyn Right. On your feet! Next stop the Stygian Trap.

(cross-fade plink-plonk to running stream)

Hank So this is the Stygian Trap? I expected something more sinister.

Mervyn Well, the stream's low today; in fact today it isn't a trap at all. See there; headroom for swimming!

Donald Headroom! I wonder if that's so all the way.

Mervyn As far as I can see with this torch. It's because we've had so little rain lately. Now, boys, the plan is this. I'll swim through with this line: if it's too far to shout I'll communicate by jerking. The usual code. Clear?

Donald Clear. The usual code.

Hank Clear, Mervyn.

Mervyn When I'm through –

Donald I follow?

Mervyn No, Hank will follow.

Hank Right, Mervyn.

Mervyn And I warn you: that water's icy.

Donald Well, good luck, Mervyn.

Hank Good luck.

Mervyn See you later, boys. Right. Wet hand and tilt!
(heavy splash and noise of swimmer receding – then stream running as before – fade out – pause – and fade up again)

Donald He's been gone a long time. No tug on the line even yet?

Hank Not the shadow of a tickle. Donald, what ought we to do?

Donald We'll just have to wait. Try calling again.

Hank *(calling)* Mervyn! . . . Mervyn! . . . Can you hear me?
(pause)
I think I'll go through myself.

Donald He'll murder you if you do that. We've got to wait till he tells us.

Hank But supposing he doesn't?

Donald Don't suppose things like that, Hank.
(pause: sudden increase of stream noise – and build behind)
Hank! Do you hear what I hear?

Hank My God! It must be raining outside.

Donald Is the stream higher?

Hank I'm just trying to check. I noticed a funny bit of crystal in there in the wall of the tunnel – No, my God, it's submerged!

Donald The water can rise very quickly in these places.

Hank *(calling)* Mervyn! . . . Mervyn! . . . Mervyn!
Donald, I'm going through.

Donald No, let me.

Hank I was to follow, Mervyn said.

Donald Right then, but watch yourself. If you can't get through –

Hank I'll get through. But obviously, with all this noise, we can't communicate by shouting.

Donald That's all right, I'll take over the line. Where is it?'

Hank The line? . . . Good God, it must have been swept away.

Donald Then you won't be able to communicate.

Hank Well, that's my fault isn't it? I had it in my hand.

Donald Hank, you know something? You may get through from here because you'll be swimming down stream. But how once the river's in spate could you possibly swim back against it –

Hank I used to swim for my county.

Donald Well, even so. . . All *I* can do then is wait.

Hank 'They also serve,' like the man said. See you later, Donald.

Donald Good luck, Hank.

(*violent splash*)

(*calling*) Good luck, Hank!

(*cross-fade to telephone ringing: receiver lifted*)

Police Officer . . . Yes, this is the police station. . . What! Two men cut off in a cave? And the entrance is flooding rapidly? What cave is it? . . . Skrimshank's? Never heard of it. . . Right, we'll pick you up and you'll lead us there.

(*pause: fade up*)

(*Hank humming against stream background – gradually lose latter*)

Hank (*humming*) Have you seen the life-line man, the life-line man, the life-line man – Eh? It's gone quiet – by comparison. Rain must have stopped outside. Perhaps Mervyn could hear me now. (*calling*) Mervyn! . . . Mervyn! . . . Can you hear me?

(*pause*)

So you're there! Thank God for that! Are you all right, Mervyn?

(*pause*)

Not broken anything?

(*pause*)

Fine. Then you can climb up to me. I'm up here on a ledge, miles above the water, it's safe, we can both wait here till it subsides.

(*pause*)

You don't know how to find me? I'm sorry. My battery's gone – can't think why – but light after all is not of primary importance! If you just follow my voice – it's an easy climb, but you must hurry. Right, Mervyn. Are you coming? (*pause*)

Mervyn, are you coming?

(*pause*)

You answered just now – or did you answer just now?

(*to self*) No, Hank you fool, he didn't answer just now. That's what's called wishful thinking.

Hallucinations. But not due to alcohol. No, Doctor Butler, truly. I took my pill this morning, I've never lapsed once, Doctor Butler. But I've just thought of something funny: Doctor Butler, you look like a butler.

Doctor (*as butler*) Herr Professor Lidebrock.

Hank Oh, my dear Professor, I've always wanted to meet you, since my mother used to read me your adventures. How you went down the volcano and ran into all those mastodons. But, of course, in your case you got out again.

Professor That was because I am a character in fiction.

Hank I'd forgotten that! So you are.

Professor Jules Verne invented me. But who, mein Herr, invented you?

Doctor Mr Jim White of Texas.

White That you, Hank? What you doing in that little rat-hole, buddy? Why can't you get you a man-sized cave like I did? It's got two elevators now – cost a hundred and sixty thousand bucks. And a male voice choir on record. State of New Mexico gave me a book-stall down there. Most subterranean bookstall in the world. Sells only one book – mine: all about the Carlsbad and how I dis-covered it. Way it came about was when the bats flew out.

Hank (*humming*) Bats in the Carlsbad,

        Bats in the belfry,

        Bats in –

(*speaking*) Bats in my bloody stomach! When did I last have a meal?

Doctor Mrs Beeton.

Hank Ah, Mrs Beeton! 'What feast is toward in thine eternal cell?' Not soya link sausage again, I hope? We had enough of that in Burma.

Mrs Beeton Take five dozen eggs and a thirty pound turkey, an armful of parsley and a pinch of gypsum –

Doctor An Officer who has been Attempting to get in Touch with You.

Bailiff Mr Hankey! How nice to meet you again. The circumstances are not as propitious as last time and I fear they have sent me to dis-train on this cave. Unless the little lady with the cash –

Hank She's not here!

Bailiff In that case I must make an inventory. Perhaps you'd be so kind as to tell me which are the tools of your trade. What about these stalactites and stalagmites? Oh, and this hour-glass?

Hank Don't you dare touch that! That's what I've got to beat.

Doctor Pablo Picasso.

Hank And about time, too. I've a bone to pick with you, Pablo. You may be a genius but you've done us wrong. Grievous spiritual harm. You set us all doodling when we should have been painting pictures. And why are you not wearing your diving suit? After all, Salvador Dali did.

Bailiff Excuse me, Mr Hankey, but, talking of bones, I've just found some. Am I right in assuming that, if they're prehistoric –

Doctor The Red Lady of Paviland.

Red Lady Here I come, dancing all in my bones –

Hank Don't wobble like that. It's bad animation.

Red Lady In my old red bones all made up with ruddle. Dr Buckland found me in Goat's Cave down in the Gower Peninsula. I was the only lady there, the others were all riff-raff – bears and hyenas –

Hank Come off it, you're no lady. You're a Cro-Magnon Man.

Doctor The Emperor Friedrich Barbarossa.

Barbarossa Tief im Schosse des Kyffhäusers
bei der Ampel rotem Schein
sitzt der alte Kaiser Friedrich
an dem Tisch aus Marmelstein.
I am returned from my cave to redeem my people.

Hank You hear this fellow in the cellarage?
We're not your people, Emperor. Go and wear your new clothes somewhere else.

Doctor Corporal Hokusai Hirosaki.

Jap Lieutenant Hankey, I presume?

Hank Yes, Corporal.

Jap You should have waited.

Hank Waited for what?

Jap You should have killed me later. Or not at all.

Hank Or not at all. But, truly, I never expected to hit you.

Jap It is a pity. I was an artist too.

Doctor Mrs Hankey, mother of the accused.

Mother My long-lost boy! It seems an age since I've seen you.

Hank Only some thirty-five years.

142

Mother Still I saw your little girl-friend: pretty in her way. She gave me some lovely gin. Have you got some lovely gin?

Hank Certainly not. I promised Dr Butler. And Sarah.

Bailiff If there's any gin in this cave, I'm afraid I'll have to distrain on it.

Mother Well, never mind: I had a couple before I came. But *I've* brought *you* a present. All the way from Venezuela.

Hank What is it, mother?

Mother A bar of marzipan.

Hank (*screams*)

Doctor A Person –
    (*Hank stops screaming*)
    A Person . . . from Porlock.

Hank Not another!

Person Another – yes. But the last one.

Hank Haven't I seen you before somewhere? Of course I have: I painted you.

Person In black on black. And not a bad likeness. How do you like my dark zone?

Hank I like it all right but it's taken Mervyn.

Person I've taken Mervyn.

Hank Just like a person from Porlock. Always interrupting things.

Person But what have I interrupted? I thought I'd arrived on cue. Mervyn cued me first. Then you.

Hank I don't know what you're talking about.

Person No? It's the first time, I must admit, I've had an appointment in Skrimshank's. But in many other caves and pots, none of which now you will ever visit –

Hank Why? I'm not too old.

Person People have invited me along and I always make a point of being there. In the Bertorelli Chasm, in Wookey Hole, in the Grotte du Nirzou, in the Trou de la Creuse – excuse my accent, it's because I come from Porlock – in the Gouffre de la Pierre-St-Martin, in the Font-Estramar resurgence. And now, for the first time, in Skrimshank's. Your friend Mervyn was a man after my heart.

Hank Was?

Person Was.

Hank And me?

Person Till just the other day I had my doubts about you. You made too many excuses. Still, in the end you behaved well to Sarah.

Hank I love Sarah.

Person And the day before yesterday you swam through after Mervyn.

Hank The day before yesterday? I swam through today.

Person What did Mervyn say? There's no time in these places.

Hank Anyhow, I said I'd get through and I have.

Person Yes, you have – in more senses than one. The ironic thing is: this will sell your pictures.

Hank (*yawning*) Why? I don't understand.

Person You're sleepy, aren't you?

Hank I'm glad it will sell them – if there's anything in them.

Person Of course there's something in them.

Hank Thank you. But tell me – before I drop off – why is this going to sell them?

Person Because they will say he met a noble – well, a noble person from Porlock.